D1306970

QUICK PATCHWORK PROJECTS

QUICK PATCHWORK PROJECTS

ABIGAIL BARBIER

WARD LOCK

For Orlando, Hugo, Theo and Annarose

A WARD LOCK BOOK

First published in the UK 1997
by Ward Lock
Wellington House
125 Strand
LONDON
WC2R 0BB

A Cassell Imprint

Distributed in the United States
by Sterling Publishing Co., Inc.
387 Park Avenue South, New York, NY 10016–8810

A British Library Cataloguing in Publication Data block for this book may be obtained from the British Library

ISBN 0 7063 7562 9
Designed by Ian Hunt Design
Illustrations by Kate Simunek
Photography by Amanda Heywood
Edited by Lydia Darbyshire
Printed and bound in Hong Kong by Colorcraft

ACKNOWLEDGEMENTS

The author and publishers would like to thank the following companies for supplying fabrics used in projects in this book: Laura Ashley (Beach Bag, Picnic Rug, Evening Star Double Quilt and Drawing Room Throw), Liberty & Co. (Trip Around the World Cot Quilt and Diamond-in-a-square Wall Hanging) and Ciel Décor (Provençal Tablecloth). All the companies have a mail order service and can be contacted as follows:

LAURA ASHLEY
Customer Services
P.O. Box 19
Newtown
Powys
SY16 1DZ
Tel: 01686 622116

LIBERTY RETAIL LIMITED
210–220 Regent Street
London
WIR 6AH
Tel: 0171 573 9445
or 0171 734 1234

CIEL DÉCOR
187 New King's Road
London
SW6 4SW
Tel: 0171 731 0444

CONTENTS

Introduction 6
Materials, Equipment and Techniques 7

THE PROJECTS
Overnight Bag 16
Evening Bag 22
Beach Bag 25
Rucksack 28
Make-up Bag 32
Waistcoat 35
Sleeveless Jacket 38

Child's Skirt 44
Little Purse 48
Scrunchy 50
Hairband 51
Little House Picture 53
Tea Cosy 56
Egg Cosy 58
Place Mat 60
Provençal Tablecloth 62
Log Cabin Cushion 67
Crazy Patchwork Cushion 70
Doll's Shoofly Quilt 72
Picnic Rug 76
Drawing Room Throw 79
Ohio Star Single Quilt 82
Log Cabin Throw 85
Nine-patch Single Quilt 89
Kilim Wall Hanging 92
Evening Star Double Quilt 96
Square-in-the-middle Single Quilt 101
Diamond-in-a-square Wall Hanging 104
Trip Around the World Cot Quilt 108
Amish Wall Hanging 111
Ocean Waves Double Quilt 116
English Medallion Quilt 122

Index 128

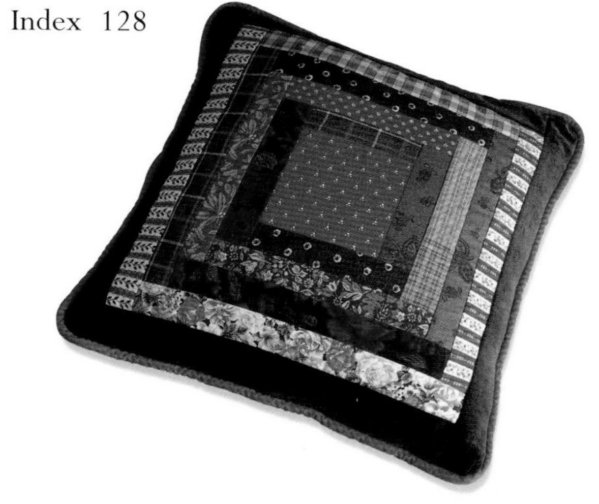

INTRODUCTION

My love of patchwork began when I was given a handmade patchwork quilt as a wedding present. Sadly, because the fabrics used were thin, it soon became worn, and I decided to replace it. I spent every evening for a week cutting up bits of material and old clothes, laying them out on the bed and creating a design that I liked. It was such a thrill to see how patterns and colours changed when they were juxtaposed with one another and how the design suddenly fell into place and 'felt right'. The resulting quilt ended up on the kitchen wall, so another quilt had to be made for the bed; then the children needed one; then friends wanted one; then commissions started coming in . . . and so it went on!

The idea for this book came because I wanted to share with others how easily – and how quickly – a quilt can be made. I have four children, so my sewing has to be done in short bursts, and projects must not take too long to complete or interest and impetus are lost and they remain in my work-basket indefinitely. This book is, therefore, intended for people who have little time but who still want to create something with their own hands or their sewing-machine. Lack of time and self-confidence and the fact that most of us go out to work or work in the home may mean that our creative impulses do not have an outlet. But it is possible to produce something beautiful but that is easy to make in an hour or at most a weekend, and there is nothing as satisfying as completing a piece of handiwork and exhibiting it on the wall or bed for all to admire.

The centuries-old craft of patchwork involves the bringing together of scraps of fabric to create something new out of something old. Like many crafts, patchwork was born of necessity, and necessity brought creativity, and now quilts are recognized as an art form. Many of the designs for quilts included in this book were inspired by nineteenth-century American and English patchworks, and in keeping with that period, the equipment used has been kept to the minimum. To give your quilts a greater sense of authenticity, use cast-off clothes or old sheets and blankets where appropriate. One of the joys of contemplating a quilt or wall hanging is the associations that each piece of material that has been used brings to mind – an old summer dress will be a reminder of sunny childhood days, flowery curtains from a redecorated bedroom will recall the former furnishings, or the pyjamas that are no longer needed by a now gangly, teenage youth will be a constant memento of the toddler who wore them.

The choice of colours and patterns of the fabrics used in this book is entirely my own personal taste, and it was often dictated by what was available at the time. Do not feel that you must stick to these colourways. You are free to use any materials you wish, as long as you use similar weight fabrics together. Remember that changing the positions of light and dark textiles can dramatically change the overall visual impact of a quilt, so experiment with different colours and tones by laying fabrics next to one another and cutting a few pieces first to see how the shades work together. Once you have chosen your materials – which is probably the most difficult but also the most creative part of patchwork – you will be ready to begin. So put your foot down on the sewing-machine pedal and get going!

Materials, Equipment and Techniques

FABRICS

Unless otherwise specified, use 100 per cent dress-weight cotton fabrics for all the projects in this book. Cotton is easier to sew and is more authentic, because most old American quilts were made using cotton. There are many different types of cotton fabric available, including lawn, corduroy, gingham, chambray and velvet, all of which have been used in this book.

It is not essential to buy new fabrics: old clothes or sheets can be used, as long as the templates are not cut out of obviously worn parts, and it is much more enjoyable to look at a quilt that is made up of materials that bring back fond memories. Always wash and iron new fabrics before you use them to test for colour fastness and shrinkage.

The fabric amounts given in the projects are for 115cm (44in) wide material, unless otherwise specified. If the fabric that you choose is wider or narrower, adjust the amount accordingly, using the method given below.

Provençal Tablecloth

ESTIMATING FABRIC LENGTHS

Work out the number of patches that will fit across the width of the fabric, then divide the total number of patches needed by this number. Multiply this figure by the length of the patch to give the quantity of material required.

For example, the preparation list for the Nine-patch Single Quilt specifies 60 navy squares measuring 12 x 12cm (4¾ x 4¾in). If the fabric is 90cm (36in) wide, 7 squares will fit across (90 divided by 12 or 36 divided by 4¾). Now divide the total number of patches needed by this figure (60 divided by 7 = 8). Multiply this figure by the length of the patch (8 x 12 = 96 or 8 x 4¾ = 38). You will need 1m (96cm rounded up) or 38in of fabric.

The same method applies to sashes and borders. To make the Tea and Egg Cosies, which use an equilateral triangle template, divide the width of fabric by the patch measurement (90 divided by 9cm = 10 or 36 divided by 3½ = 10). Double this figure and take away 1 (10 x 2 = 20 - 1 = 19). This gives you the number of triangles that will fit into one another across the fabric. Proceed as before to get the length of the fabric required.

Remember that you must use either metric or imperial measurements. The equivalent measurements are not interchangeable.

EQUIPMENT

It is not necessary to buy expensive equipment for making patchworks, and the items you will need have been kept to the minimum for the purposes of this book. The following is all that you will require:

For sewing:

- a sharp pair of dressmaking scissors
- small pointed embroidery scissors (a scissor sharpener is useful)
- rotary cutter (optional)
- a sewing machine with forward and backward stitch function (buttonholes and zigzag/satin stitch are useful but not essential)
- unpicker
- ruler (30cm/12in)
- tape measure or long metal rule (1m/36in)
- quilting pins (these are extra long with glass heads)
- sewing needles
- machine needles for thick, medium and thin fabrics
- water-soluble fabric marker or felt-tip pen if the marks will not be visible

For templates:

- ruler
- graph paper in either centimetre or inch squares
- compass
- card or plastic
- pencils
- rubber
- sharpener
- glue stick
- craft knife (optional)

MAKING THE TEMPLATES

If you have access to a photocopier, enlarge the templates by the percentage indicated. Enlarge by 200%, for example, indicates that the template should be twice the size given. If you prefer, draw your own on graph paper, stick onto card and cut out.

To make an equilateral triangle template, draw the base on graph paper, open a compass to the same length and, with the point of the compass at one end of the base, make a small arc. Repeat with the compass at the other end. Draw two lines, meeting where arcs intersect.

Window templates are required when you need to centre a fabric motif on a patch. Make it in the same way as a normal template, but cut out the centre, leaving a 1cm (½in) border. To make a diamond window template (as for the Overnight Bag) draw two equilateral triangles as above but sharing the same base. Draw a line 1cm (½in) inside the outside edge. Stick to card and cut around the outside line and then cut out the centre up to the inside line (Fig. 1). Otherwise, make a template out of perspex.

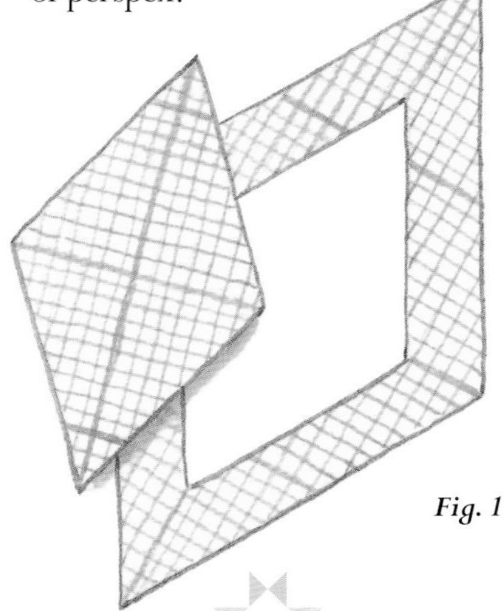

Fig. 1

Overnight Bag

THREADS AND STITCHES

Use 100 per cent cotton or polyester thread, but make sure the bobbin contains the same type of thread as the spool on your machine.

To sew patches together, use a stitch length of 6 stitches to 1cm (7 stitches to ½in). For quilting, use a longer machine stitch of 4 stitches to 1cm (5 stitches to ½in).

The term top-stitching is used to denote stitching a fabric down on the right side with the raw edge folded under.

Zigzag stitching is sometimes required, as in the English Medallion Quilt, for appliquéd designs. If you do not have this option on your machine, either omit the design altogether or apply iron-on interfacing, which will prevent the edges of the fabric to be appliquéd from fraying. The pieces can then be hand sewn with a slip stitch or machine sewn with a straight stitch in place.

TECHNIQUES

CUTTING

Lay the template on the straight grain of the fabric and cut one, two or even three layers at a time. If the grain of the fabric is straight, it is possible to tear long strips the same width as your square template and then cut across the strips, using the template. Make a 1cm (½in) cut into the selvedge and quickly and firmly tear across the width of the material (Fig. 2). This is a particularly useful technique for needlecord, which tears very easily down the grain, and also for all the strip-pieced projects.

PIECING

All piecing of patches must be done with fabrics right sides together, unless otherwise specified. Pin pieces together with pins at right angles to the seam, then machine stitch 6mm (¼in) from the raw edge, slowing down as you go over the pins, and backstitching a few stitches at the start and end of each patch (Fig. 3).

A quick way of sewing several pairs of patches together is to sew them in a chain without cutting the thread between them. Once all the pieces have been stitched, snip them apart (Fig. 4).

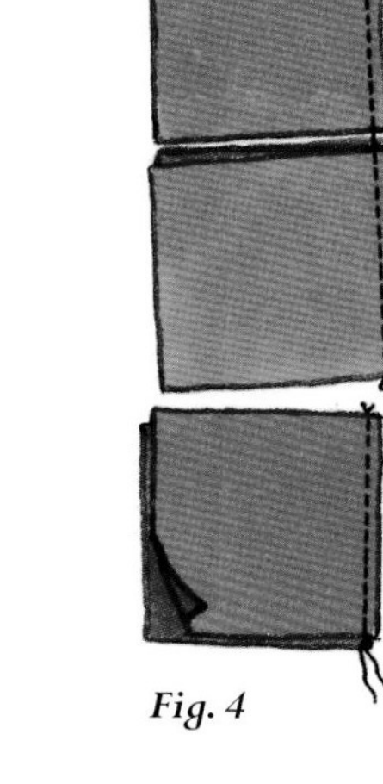

Fig. 2

Fig. 3

Fig. 4

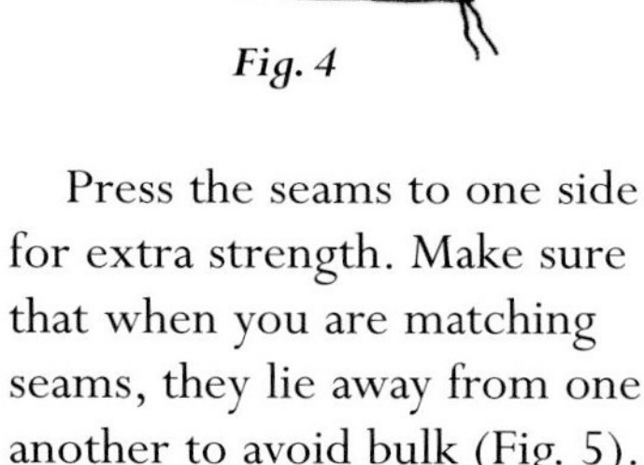

Press the seams to one side for extra strength. Make sure that when you are matching seams, they lie away from one another to avoid bulk (Fig. 5).

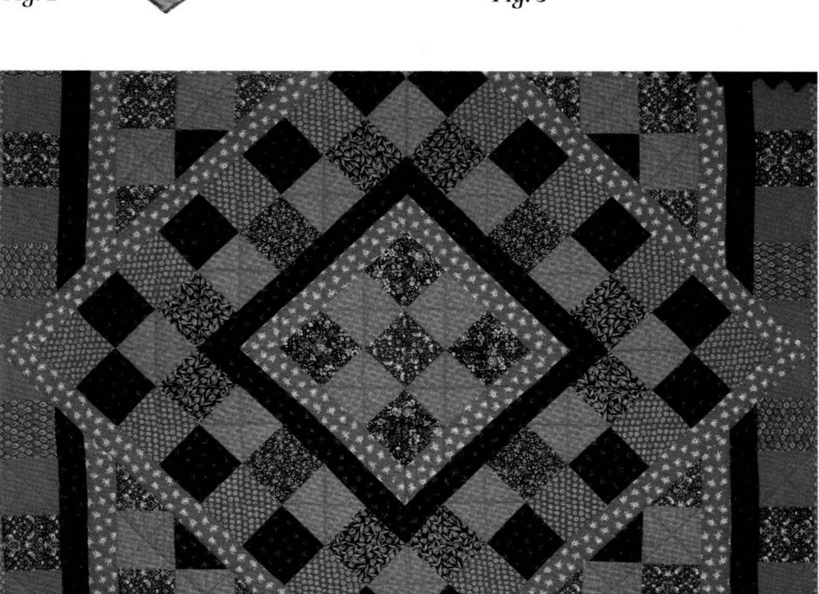

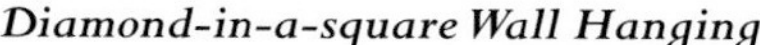

Diamond-in-a-square Wall Hanging

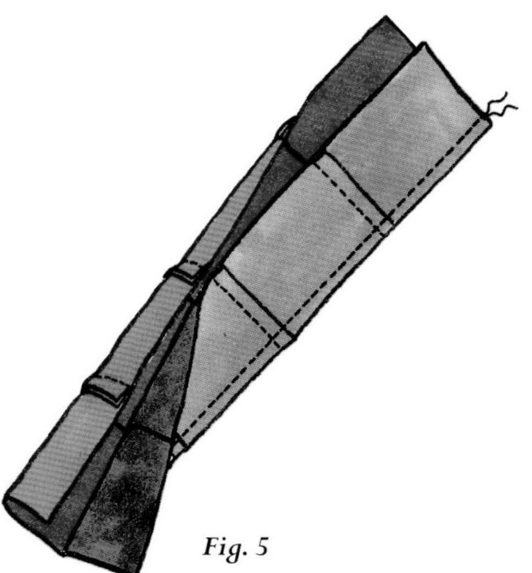

Fig. 5

When you are joining different angles and oblique angles together, position the patches so that the ends of the seam allowance meet rather than the corners of the patches (Fig. 6).

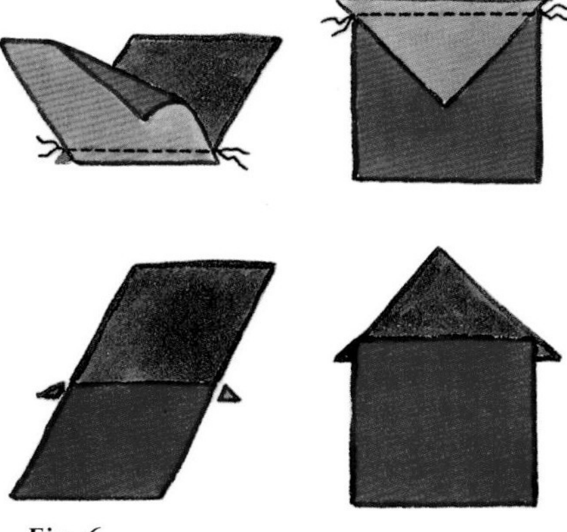

Fig. 6

Sometimes you will find that the seams of two pieced sections do not quite match. When this happens, pin the seams together and, with the shorter pieced section uppermost, slowly stitch along the seam line, pulling a little on the top fabric to help it to fit. In this way you will find that even a 6mm (¼in) per 8cm (3in) patch discrepancy can be eased away (Fig. 7). However, it does not matter too much if pieces do not match exactly. It is the irregularities in a quilt that add to its charm and uniqueness – as long, of course, as these irregularities are not too glaringly obvious.

PRESSING

It is essential to press the fabrics before they are used and after sewing every seam. Make sure that when a seam meets another seam, they lie in opposite directions (see Fig. 5).

When the patchwork is complete, press it thoroughly before placing it on top of the wadding/batting and backing. Then, once it is on the wadding, press it very lightly to remove any folds before pinning.

BACKING FABRIC

Because the backing fabric is not going to be seen very often, economize by using old sheets or lightweight cotton curtains to back the quilts. If the sheet is not wide enough, sew two together. Lay the patchwork on top and cut the backing 5–10cm (2–4in) bigger than the patchwork all the way round.

WADDING/BATTING

All the projects included in this book have used medium thickness polyester wadding/batting, which is 6mm (¼in) thick or sold by weight as 100gm (4oz). The wadding/batting comes in 1m (39in) widths and so will normally need to be joined together to make a piece wide enough for a single or double patchwork quilt. To join wadding/batting, overlap the edges to be joined by 1cm (½in) and sew along the length, using a long zigzag or basting stitch (Fig. 8). Wadding/batting should be cut 5cm (2in) larger than the patchwork top – that is, slightly smaller than the backing.

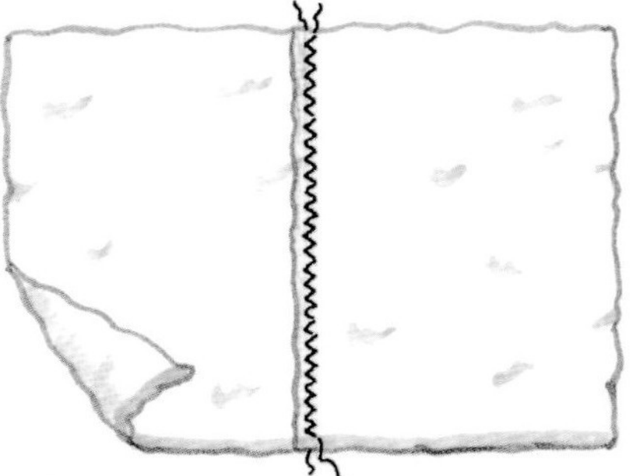

Fig. 8

It is possible to obtain cotton wadding or wool wadding, and although these are more faithful to the quilt-making tradition, they are perhaps less convenient since they may not be machine washable.

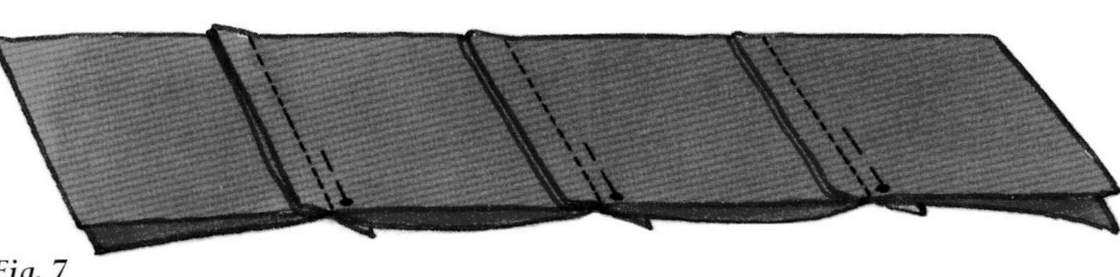

Fig. 7

Trip Around the World Cot Quilt

QUILTING

Quilting can be worked along seam lines of pieced patches – 'in the ditch' (Fig. 9) – as in the Evening Star Quilt or diagonally across patches (Fig. 10), as in the Cot Quilt. Alternatively, the quilting itself can form a design (Fig. 11), as in the Amish Wall Hanging.

Fig. 9

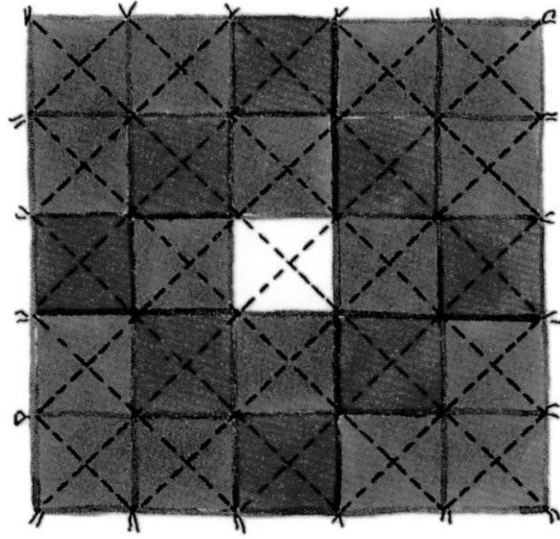

Fig. 10

Fig. 11

Lay the backing fabric the wrong side up and iron it lightly to remove any creases. Place the wadding/batting on top. Lay the patchwork, right side up, on top of the wadding/batting. Lightly press and smooth out any folds. Working from the centre outwards, pin through all three layers every 5–8cm (2–3in). Quilt with the pins still in place, removing them as you sew (be prepared for painful pin-pricks with this method). Alternatively, baste through all the layers with quilting thread or with double-thickness normal thread, again working from the centre outwards and making either an even grid or a spider's web effect (Fig. 12). Remove the pins and machine quilt, using a long machine stitch (4 stitches to 1cm/5 stitches to ½in) and a medium needle. Stitch the central quilting lines first, and work outwards from there. Roll up the quilt tightly to fit under the head of your machine.

To transfer a quilting design to a quilt top, as for the centre of the Amish Quilt, lay dressmaker's carbon paper face down on the right side of the fabric to be quilted. Place the design on top of the carbon and draw over the lines with a ballpoint pen or soft pencil, pressing firmly. If the lines are feint on the fabric, go over them with a coloured pencil that will show up clearly. Machine stitch over the lines in a slow and continuous movement. Quilting geometric designs is a reasonably straightforward task, but patterns with leaves and other curved lines are quite difficult to do, and they are not recommended for inexperienced quilters.

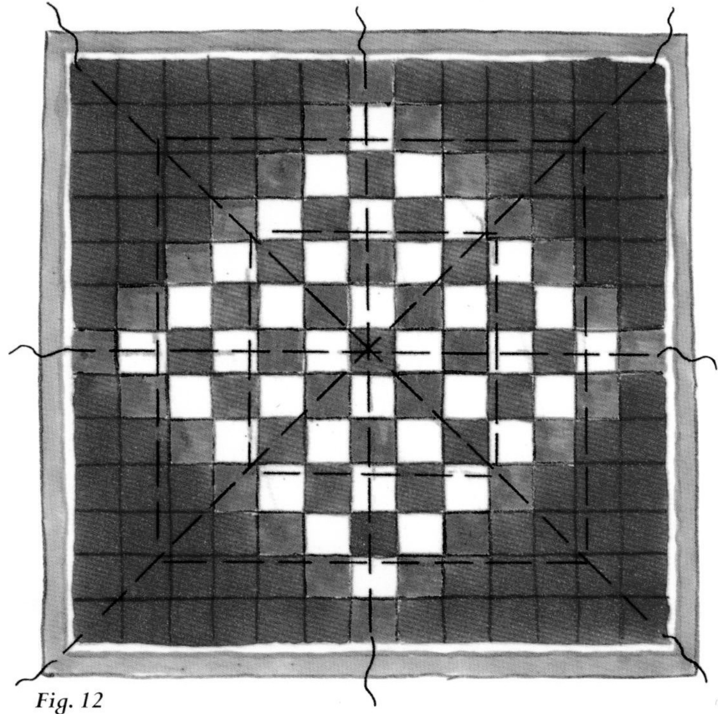

Fig. 12

BINDING

A quilt has to be bound to cover the raw edges, and three different methods are used in this book. The first is called self-binding, in which the quilt backing is folded over to the front, as with the Drawing Room Throw, or the quilt top is folded over to the back, as with the Log Cabin Throw.

The second method is called binding with a strip, in which a narrow strip of material is folded over the quilt's edges, as with the Square-in-the-middle Single Quilt.

In the third method, the binding itself forms part of the quilt's overall design, as with the dog-tooth border of the Diamond-in-a-square Wall Hanging.

Self-binding

To bind with the backing, trim the backing so that it overlaps the quilt evenly all the way round by at least 5cm (2in). Turn the raw edges of the backing to the wrong side by 6mm (¼in) and press (Fig. 13).

Fold the backing to the right side of the quilt to overlap raw edges by 1cm (½in) all the way round the quilt. Pin the backing in place. Mitre the corners (see page 14 for mitring), then stitch the binding in position close to the edge (Fig. 14).

To bind with the quilt top, repeat the above procedure, but this time make sure that the quilt top overlaps the backing and fold it to the back.

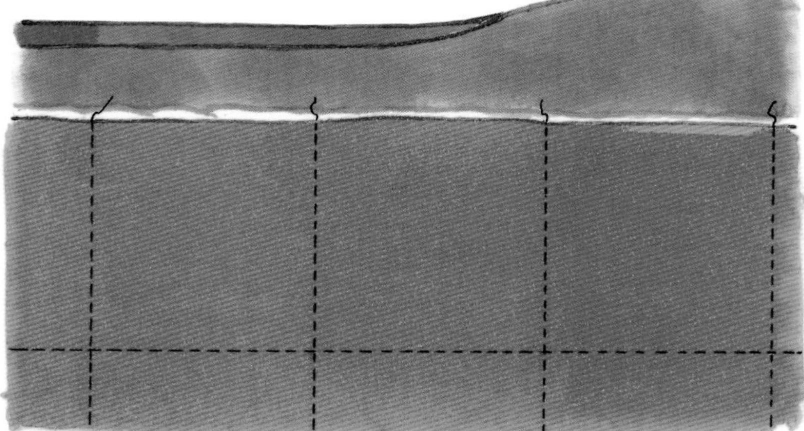

Fig. 13

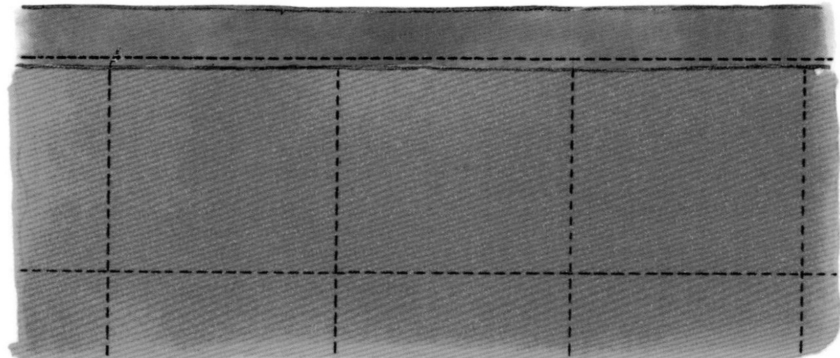

Fig. 14

English Medallion Quilt

Binding with a Strip

Cut a binding strip to the width indicated in the project and the length of the perimeter of the quilt plus 10cm (4in). Turn one long edge of the binding to the wrong side by 6mm (¼in) and press. Beginning at the centre of one side of the quilt, fold the binding end 1cm (½in) to the wrong side and pin the unpressed edge of the binding to the quilt back, matching raw edges. Stitch 6mm (¼in) from the edge (Fig. 15). When you are 6mm (¼in) away from the corner, and with the needle in the quilt, raise the presser foot and pivot the quilt around, ready to sew down the next side. Align the binding with the edge of the quilt, lower the presser foot, making sure that you do not catch the fold in the binding when stitching (see Fig. 15). When you arrive back at the beginning, continue to stitch so that the binding overlaps by 2cm (¾in) before cutting (Fig. 16). Fold the binding strip to the right side of the quilt to cover the stitching line, and overlap the raw edges by 1cm (½in). Top-stitch close to the edge. When you are using a narrow binding strip it is not necessary to mitre the corners, simply make a couple of neat tucks as you go around the quilt corner (Fig. 17).

Decorative Bindings

The above technique would also apply to decorative bindings, as in the dog-tooth border of the Diamond-in-a-square Wall Hanging (page 106).

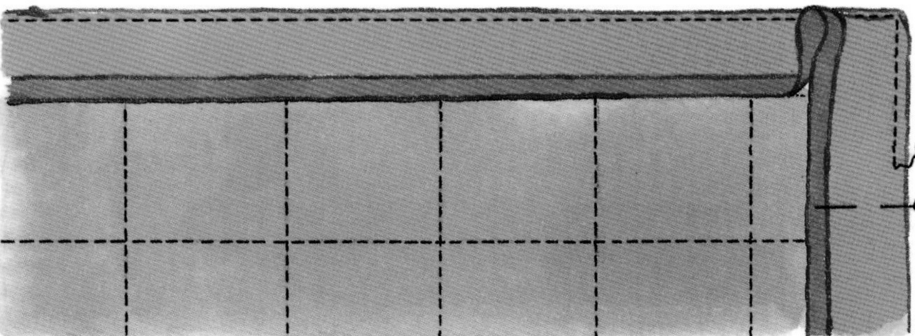

Fig. 15

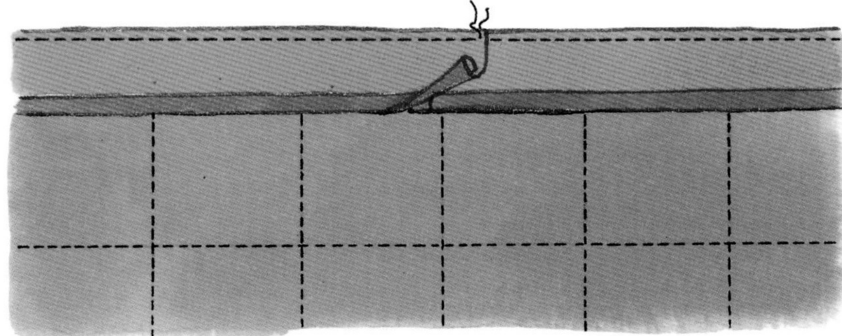

Fig. 16

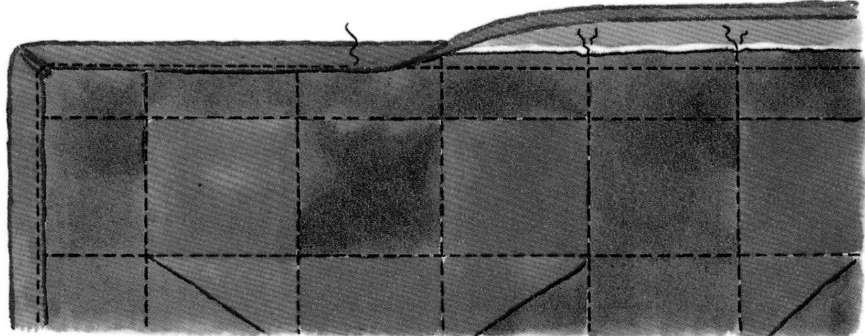

Fig. 17

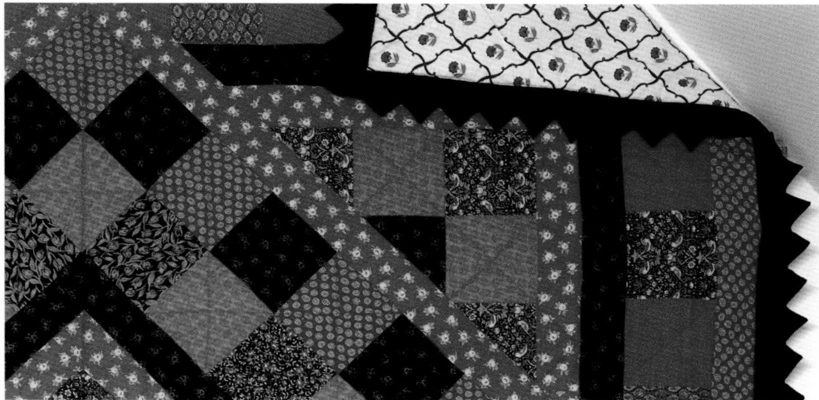

Diamond-in-a-square Wall Hanging dog-tooth border

MITRING CORNERS

Mitring the corners of a quilt binding gives a neat finish. Follow the instructions for the strip binding, tucking in the binding at the corners of the quilt top to form a 45 degree fold line. Slip stitch by hand or machine stitch forwards and backwards as you stitch around the quilt (Fig. 18).

SQUARE CORNERS

Stitch binding strips along both lengths of the quilt and trim them to the same size as the quilt. Sew binding strips across both widths, including the binding strips at both ends, and trim. Fold the binding lengths to the right side of the quilt and pin. Fold the binding widths to the right side and pin. Stitch round the edge of the binding. Stitch a cross in a square at each corner (Fig. 19).

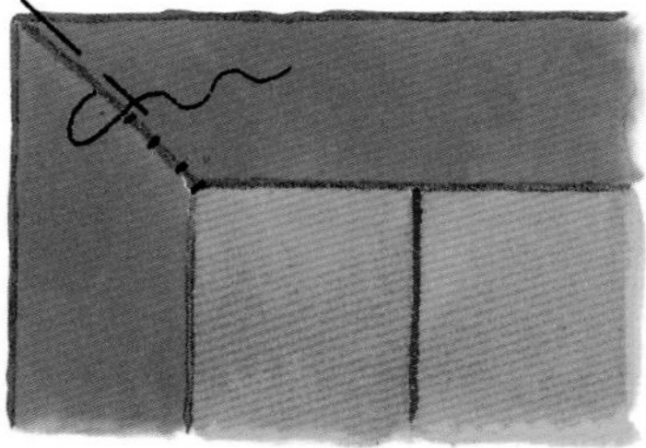

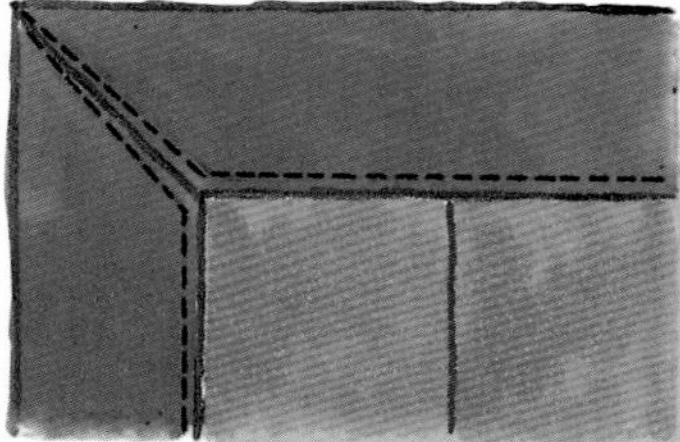

Fig. 18

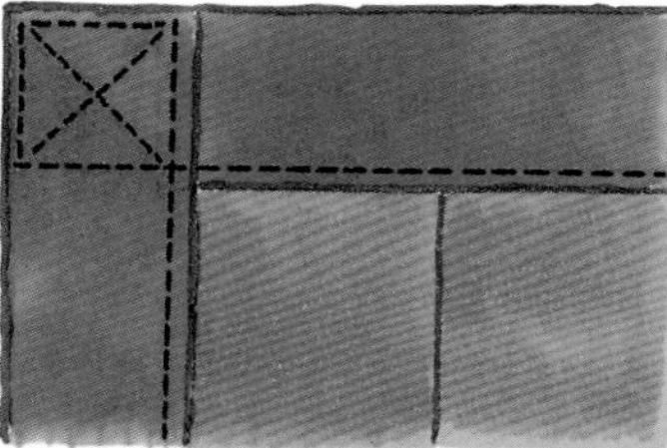

Fig. 19

SIGNING AND HANGING QUILTS

Do not forget to sign and date your quilt by embroidering your name in one corner either on the front or the back – depending how modest you are.

To hang a quilt for display, attach loops to the back of the quilt and thread them on a wooden pole. Make the loops from 5cm (2in) wide fabric cut into 15cm (6in) lengths. Fold each piece in half along the length, stitch, then turn right side out. Centre the seam and press. Fold under the raw edges of the loop ends and slip stitch to the quilt back. Attach as many loops as are necessary to support the weight of the quilt.

Kilim Wall Hanging

THE PROJECTS

Overnight Bag

This travel bag is just the right size for an overnight stay. The interfacing is optional – although it gives the bag a more solid appearance, it also makes it difficult to manoeuvre the fabric when you are sewing. The bag could be made smaller by substituting a small panel for the large central panel. If you do this, decrease the length and width of the background fabric proportionately.

Finished measurements:
58cm (23in) wide, 33cm (13in) high

MATERIALS

- 3 templates (1 diamond and 2 triangles)
- 50cm (20in) fabric A (blue floral fabric)
- 30cm (12in) fabric B (Fleur de Lys fabric)
- 25cm (10in) fabric C (beige paisley pattern on cream)
- 50cm (20in) fabric D (black geometric pattern on taupe)
- 75cm (30in) wadding/batting
- 75cm (30in) lining (canvas or herringbone weave in cream)
- 75cm (30in) stiff interfacing (optional)
- 5m (16ft 6in) webbing, 3.75cm (1½in) wide, for handles
- 55cm (22in) zip fastener
- cream thread

PREPARATION

Cut or rip the following pieces:

- **Fabric A**
  2 diamonds, cut using the template
  6 strips, each 4cm x 1m (1½ x 36in)
- **Fabric B**
  4 diamonds, cut using the template
  2 strips, each 4cm x 1m (1½ x 36in)
  2 rectangles, each 10 x 35cm (4 x 14in), for the side panels
- **Fabric C**
  3 strips, each 3cm x 1m (1¼ x 36in)
  Fold remaining fabric in half and cut 4 large triangles (i.e., 8 in all) using the template
- **Fabric D**
  2 sashes, each 60 x 10cm (24 x 4in)
  1 rectangle 60 x 20cm (24 x 8in)
  Fold remaining fabric in half and cut 8 small triangles (i.e., 16 in all) using the template

Template enlarge by 200%

To make the central panel, lay a strip of fabric C on top of the fabric A diamond, right sides together and overlapping the diamond by 2cm (¾in). Stitch.

Press the strip right side out. Line up a ruler with the edges of the diamond and lay it across the strip. Follow the line of the diamond with a water-soluble pen across the strip, then cut along the pen lines.

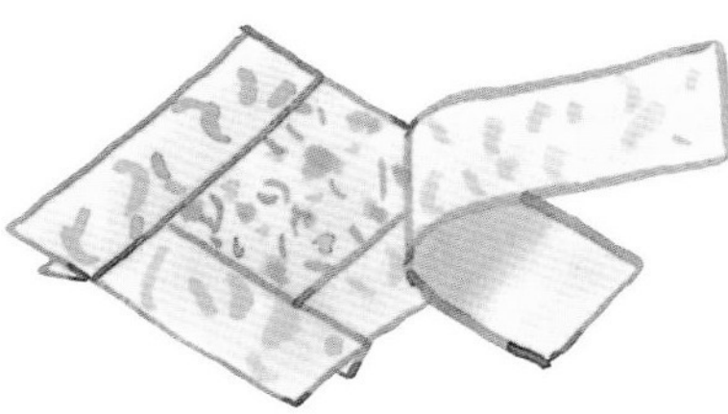

Overlap a second strip by 2cm (¾in) beyond the first strip and stitch. Trim the strip as before. Continue around the diamond, following this procedure. Sew fabric B strips around the diamond, then fabric A strips.

Sew four large triangles around the diamond to form a rectangle. Don't worry if points don't quite meet, because these will be trimmed.

Template enlarge by 200%

- **Wadding/batting**
  1 rectangle 90 x 60cm (36 x 24in)
  2 rectangles, each 10 x 35cm (4 x 14in), for the side panels
- **Lining Fabric**
  1 rectangle 90 x 60cm (36 x 24in)
  2 rectangles, each 10 x 35cm (4 x 14in), for the side panels
- **Interfacing**
  (if used)
  1 rectangle 90 x 60cm (36 x 24in)
  2 rectangles, each 10 x 35cm (4 x 14in), for the side panels

Template enlarge by 200%

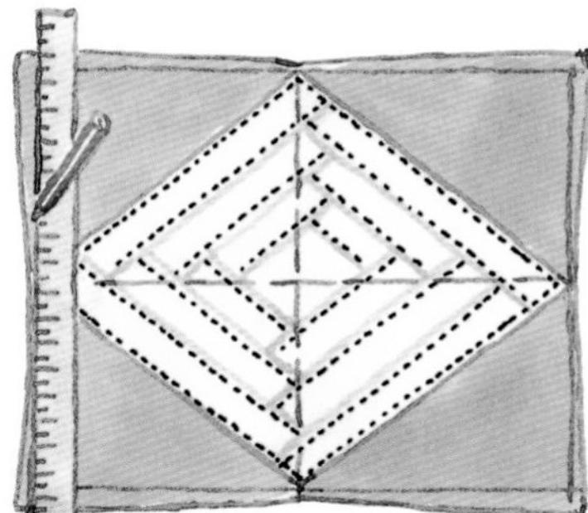

With a water-soluble pen, draw two lines on the wrong side of the rectangle through the centre of the diamond. Use these lines to measure a rectangle 31 x 21cm (12¼ x 8¼in). Trim to size. Remove pen marks with a damp cloth.

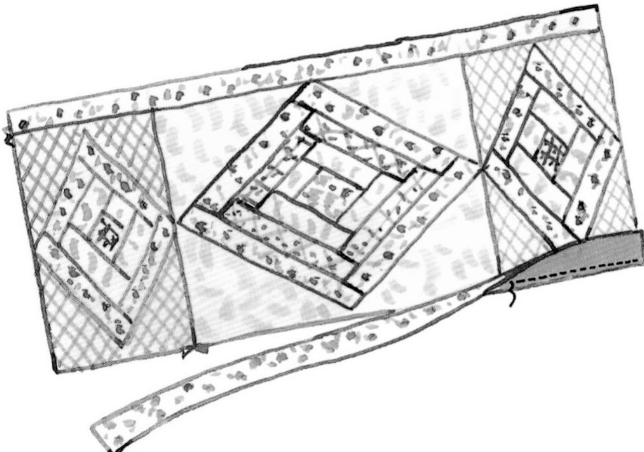

Repeat steps 1 to 5 for the second central panel. For the four smaller panels, repeat steps 1 to 5 using fabric B diamonds and omitting fabric B strips. Use the small triangles to form the rectangles. Trim the rectangles to 15 x 21cm (6 x 8¼in). Stitch a small panel on either side of each central panel. Attach fabric A strips above and below the pieced sections.

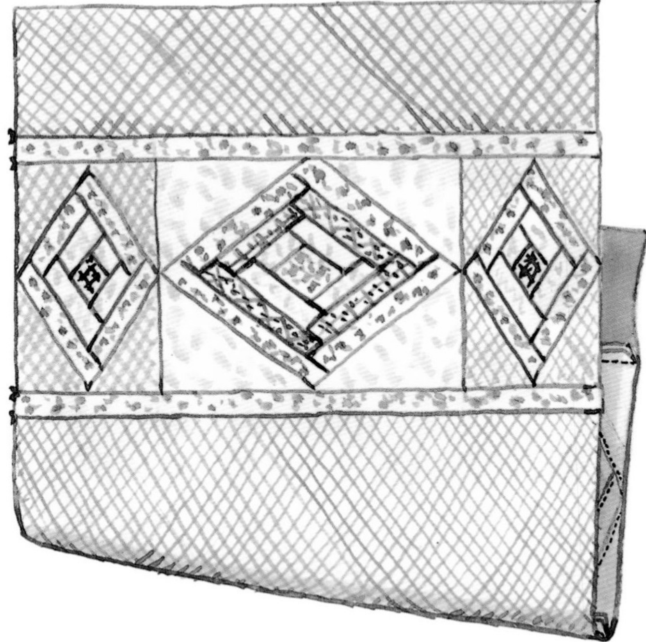

Sew fabric D sashes along the top edge of both pieced sections. Sew the fabric D 20cm (8in) piece to the bottom of one of the pieced sections. Sew the bottom edge of the remaining pieced section to the other side of the fabric D piece.

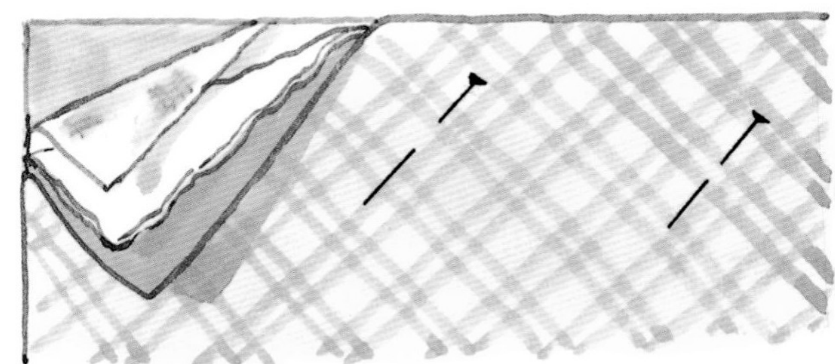

Lay the interfacing (if used) on top of the wrong side of the lining, with the wadding/batting on top of that. Place the patchwork, right side up, on top. Pin and baste securely. Trim the wadding/batting and lining.

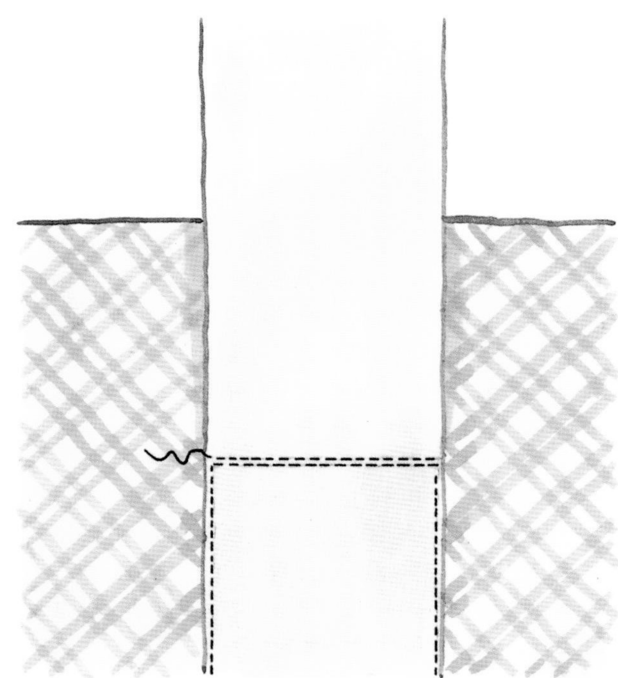

10 Pin and tack the webbing through all layers. Stitch close to both edges of the webbing, backstitching across the webbing for extra strength 4cm ($1\frac{1}{2}$in) below the top of the bag.

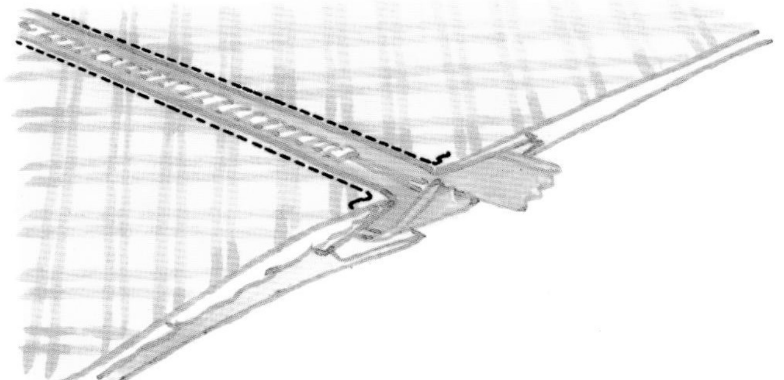

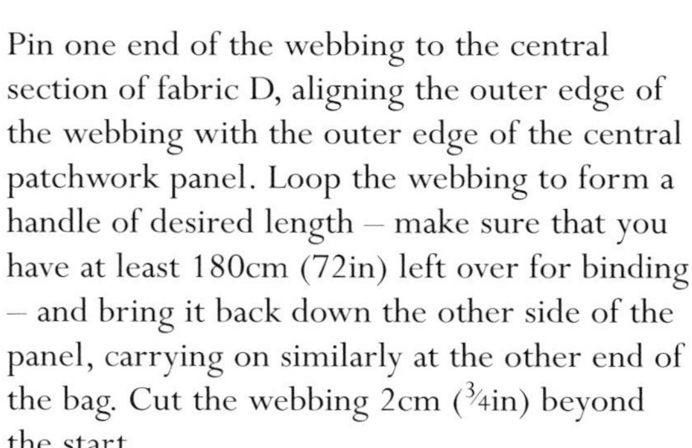

9 Pin one end of the webbing to the central section of fabric D, aligning the outer edge of the webbing with the outer edge of the central patchwork panel. Loop the webbing to form a handle of desired length – make sure that you have at least 180cm (72in) left over for binding – and bring it back down the other side of the panel, carrying on similarly at the other end of the bag. Cut the webbing 2cm ($\frac{3}{4}$in) beyond the start.

11 Fold the top edge of the right side of the bag over the wadding and interfacing (if used) by 1cm ($\frac{1}{2}$in) to the inside of the lining. Fold the right side of the lining by 1cm ($\frac{1}{2}$in) to the wrong side. Press edges. Repeat with the other side of the bag. Insert one side of the closed zip fastener between the two folded edges, butting the edges of the bag to the zip. Pin and baste, then stitch using a zipper foot. Repeat along the other side of the zip.

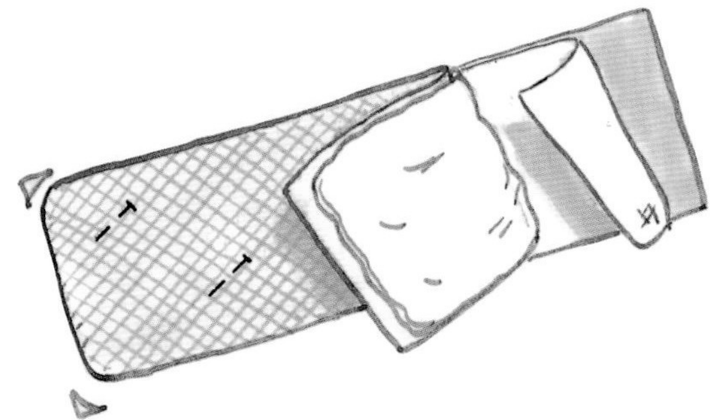

12 Lay the interfacing (if used) and the wadding/batting on top of the wrong side of the side panel lining, lay the side panel on top, right side up. Pin together. Trim the corners to round them off.

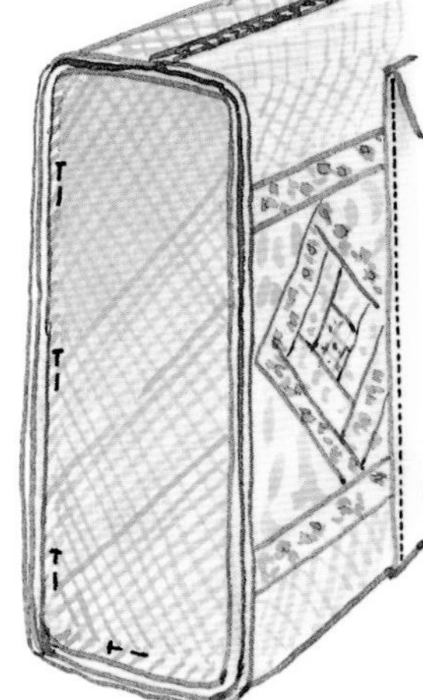

13 With linings together, centre the side panels on the bag, matching the raw edges of all layers. Pin, then baste securely.

14 Starting at the bottom of the bag, fold the webbing around the raw edges, including the zip ends, and pin. Cut the webbing 2cm ($\frac{3}{4}$in) beyond the start and fold under the raw edge. Baste, then stitch slowly, making sure that both sides of the webbing are caught. If they are not, stitch again on the other side. This part is tricky and requires patience and determination. Alternatively, bind as you would a quilt, following the instructions in the Techniques section.

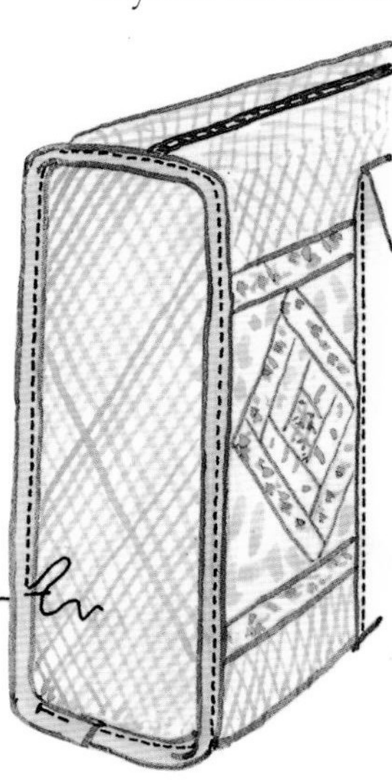

EVENING BAG

This crazy patchwork duffle bag is made out of scraps of velvet joined together with a machine embroidery stitch. If you do not have any decorative stitch functions on your machine, simply use straight stitch to join the patches and for the random stitching line.

Finished measurements:
24cm (9½in) high, 20cm (8in) wide), 5cm (2in) deep

MATERIALS

- 10cm (4in) each of black, purple, green and burgundy velvet (you can add any other scraps you may have)
- 30cm (12in) thick interfacing
- 20cm (8in) black lining fabric
- 7 11mm (⅜in) eyelets
- 150cm (60in) black rope, 7mm (¼in) thick
- reel of gold thread
- black thread

PREPARATION

Cut the following pieces:

- **Black velvet**
  1 rectangle 22 x 7cm (8¾ x 2¾in) for the base
  1 rectangle 11 x 57cm (4¼ x 22½in) for the bag lining
  1 strip 8 x 2.5cm (3 x 1in) for the rope loop
- **Interfacing**
  1 rectangle 57 x 25cm (22½ x 10in) for the bag
  1 rectangle 22 x 7cm (8¾ x 2¾in) for the base
- **Lining fabric**
  1 rectangle 18 x 57cm (7 x 22½in)
  1 rectangle 22 x 7cm (8¾ x 2¾in)

Cut two irregular pieces of different coloured velvets and lay them on the large interfacing rectangle, overlapping the two pieces. Fold under the overlapping raw edges. With gold thread in the machine and black thread in the bobbin, top-stitch with an embroidery stitch.

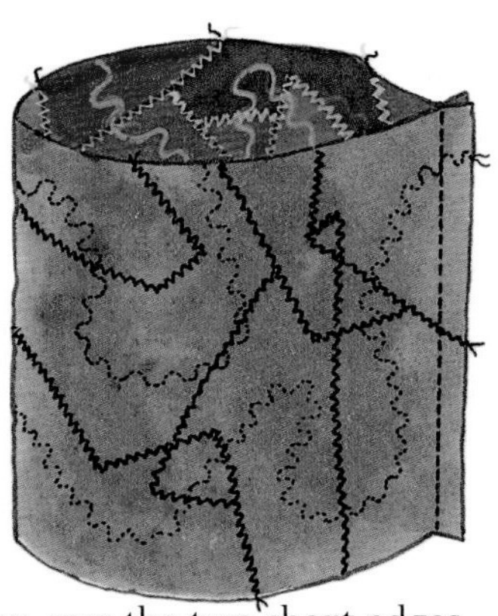

Keep adding pieces of velvet until the whole of the interfacing is covered. Sew a random stitch across the patchwork, with either a straight or decorative machine stitch. With black thread in the machine, sew the two short edges of the patchwork together, right sides together.

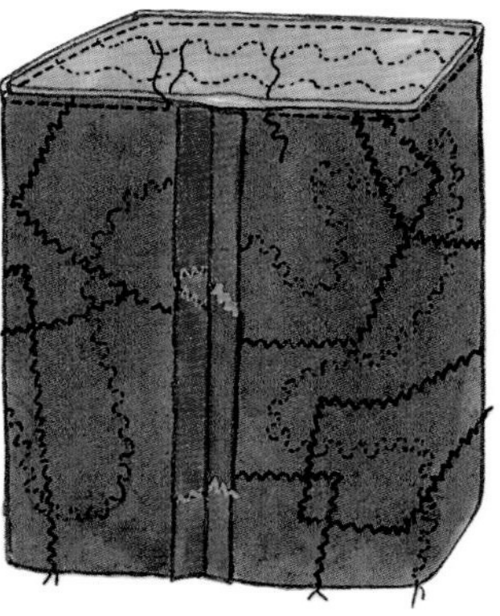

Stitch the black velvet base to the interfacing base with a decorative machine stitch. With right sides together, pin the patchwork to the base with the bag seam centred on one of the long sides of the base. Decide which side of the patchwork you want to be the back of the bag and leave a 1cm ($\frac{1}{2}$in) gap at the centre of that edge when you stitch the bag to the base.

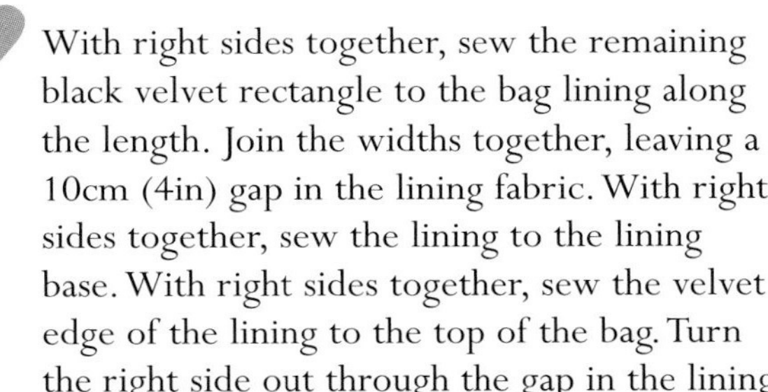

With right sides together, sew the remaining black velvet rectangle to the bag lining along the length. Join the widths together, leaving a 10cm (4in) gap in the lining fabric. With right sides together, sew the lining to the lining base. With right sides together, sew the velvet edge of the lining to the top of the bag. Turn the right side out through the gap in the lining.

Insert the eyelets, following the manufacturer's instructions, 2cm ($\frac{3}{4}$in) from the top of the bag and evenly spaced around the edge. Make sure that one eyelet is centred at the back of the bag, above the gap in the base.

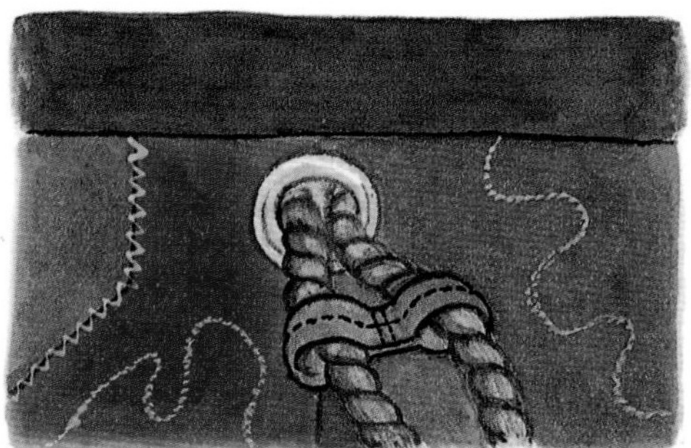

Turn under the long raw edges of the black velvet loop and top-stitch. Fold under the short raw edges, then fold the loop ends to meet in the middle of the loop. Stitch down across the widths. Insert the rope through the eyelets, with both ends coming out through the centre-back eyelet. Insert the rope ends through the loop holes.

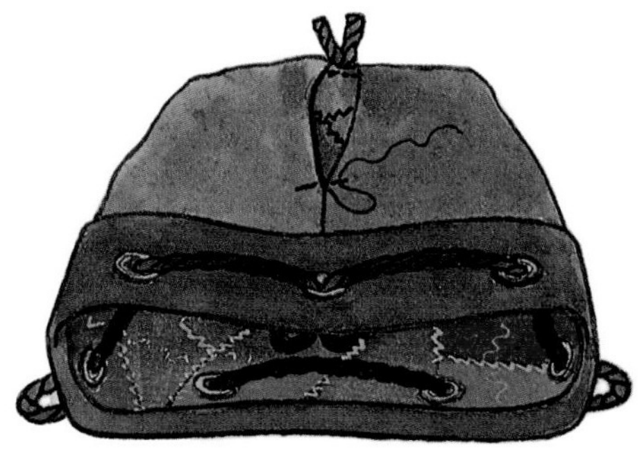

Insert the rope ends into the gap in the bag base. Turn the bag inside out and pull the base through the gap in the lining and stitch. Slip stitch the lining closed.

BEACH BAG

This bag matches the Picnic Rug (see pages 76–8), and it could be used to carry the picnic or baby accessories if the rug were used as a play pen mat.

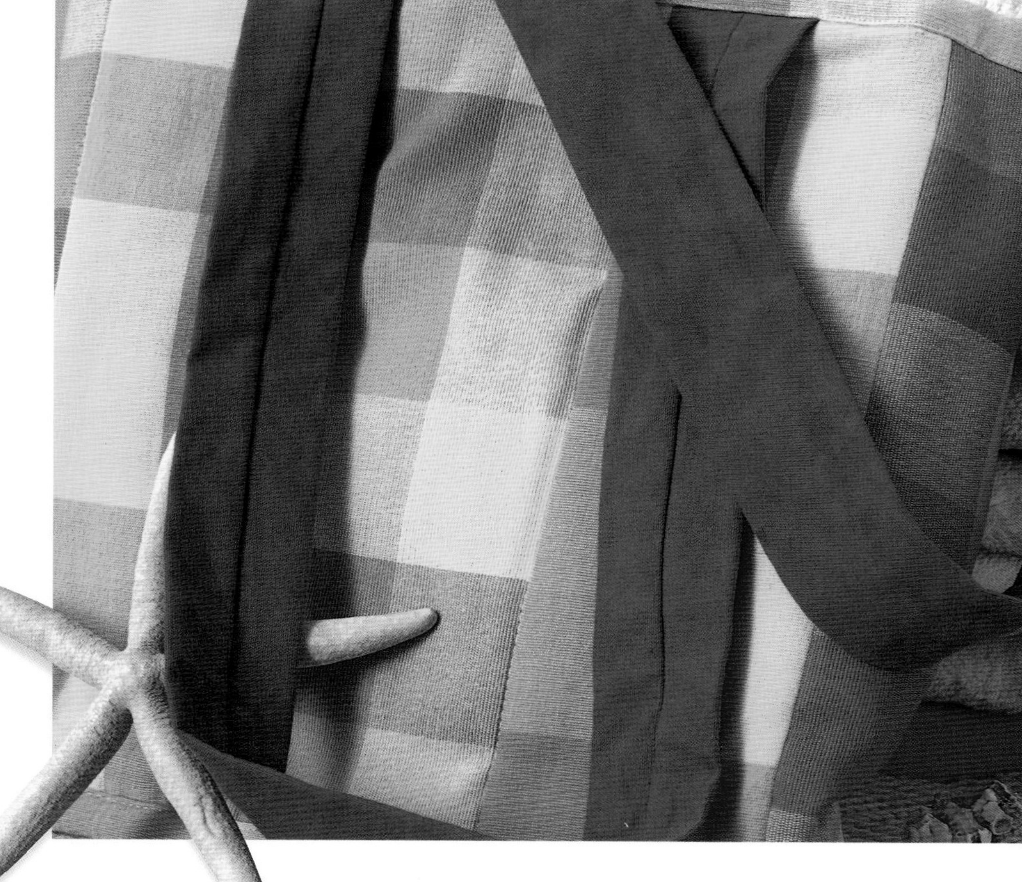

Finished measurements:
34cm (13½in) high, 41cm (16in) wide

MATERIALS

- 41cm (16in) Laura Ashley Mitford Check, deep pink
- 30cm (12in) Laura Ashley Mitford Check, chambray
- 50cm (20in) plain yellow fabric
- 41cm (16in) plain blue fabric
- 50cm (20in) wadding/batting
- yellow thread

PREPARATION

Cut the following pieces:

- **Pink check fabric**
  2 strips, each 5cm x 1m (2 x 39in), for binding
  4 rectangles, each 36 x 12cm (14 x 4¾in)
- **Chambray check fabric**
  4 rectangles, each 36 x 12cm (14 x 4¾in)
- **Yellow fabric**
  1 rectangle 88 x 38cm (34½ x 15in) for bag lining
  1 rectangle 36 x 12cm (14 x 4¾in) for base lining
- **Blue Fabric**
  1 rectangle 36 x 12cm (14 x 4¾in) for base
  2 strips, each 12 x 84cm (4¾ x 33in) for handles
- **Wadding/batting**
  1 rectangle 88 x 38cm (34½ x 15in)
  1 rectangle 36 x 12cm (14 x 4¾in)

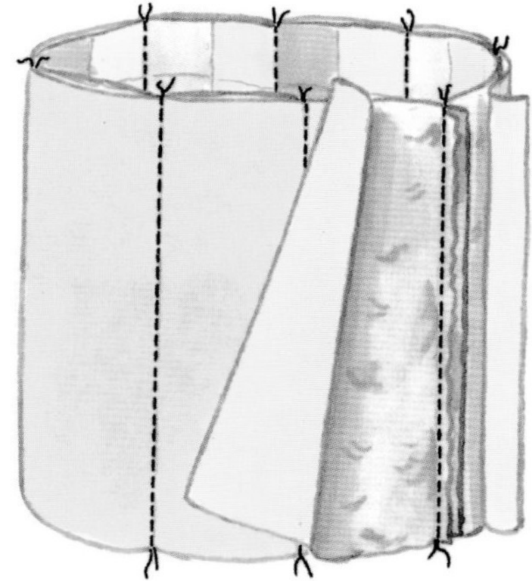

1 Sew the pink and chambray rectangles together along the long edges, alternating colours. Lay the patchwork on top of the corresponding wadding/batting and lining pieces. Pin, then quilt along the seam lines. Make a tube by folding back the lining and sewing the two short edges of the patchwork and wadding together.

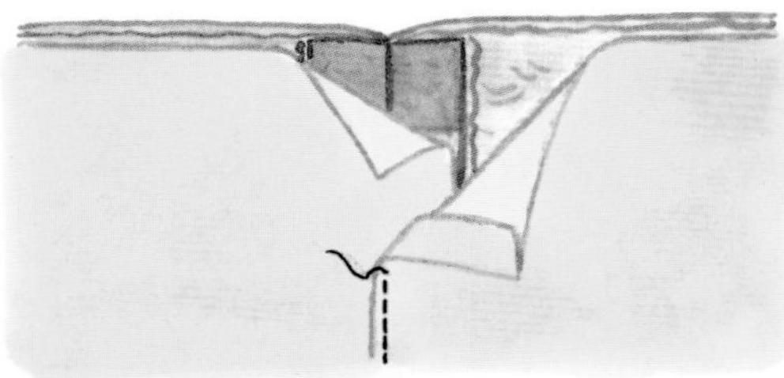

2 Cover the seam with the lining. Fold under the raw edge of the uppermost lining and topstitch in place, trying to keep the stitching along the patchwork seam line. Trim the top and bottom of the tube.

3 Quilt the bag base to the corresponding wadding/batting and lining pieces, using crisscrossing diagonal lines. Trim the corners with scissors to round them.

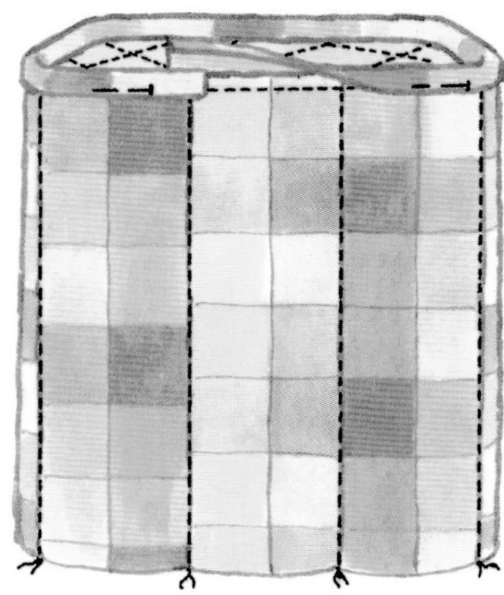

4 Pin the base to the bag with linings together. Baste in place. Bind the raw edges with the binding strip, following the instructions in the Techniques section.

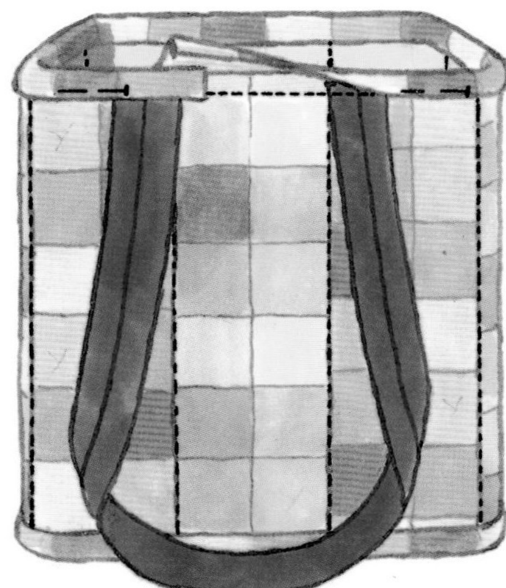

5 Fold the straps in half lengthways, right sides together, and stitch. Turn right side out and, with the seam in the middle of the underside of each strap, press. With right sides together, pin one of the strap ends to the front of the bag, matching raw edges and positioning the strap so that the ends are 10cm (4in) apart. Repeat with the other strap. Bind the top raw edge of the bag, starting behind one of the straps so that the end of the binding strip is concealed.

RUCKSACK

This rucksack was made from scraps of furnishing fabric, some taken from a sample book. These books can be bought cheaply once the patterns are discontinued. To make a child's rucksack, reduce the length of the strips by 5cm (2in) and the number of strips to 10. Adjust the straps to fit.

Finished measurements:
48cm (19in) wide, 40cm (15¾in) high

MATERIALS

- 12 strips, each 9 x 40cm (3½ x 15¾in), various upholstery fabrics (not too thick)
- 1m (1yd) fabric (can be the same as or different from the fabric used above)
- 1m (1yd) wadding/batting
- 1m (1yd) cord or rope in a coordinating colour
- 1 wooden toggle or large button
- matching thread

PREPARATION

Cut the following pieces:

- **Patterned fabric**
  1 rectangle 40 x 95cm (15¾ x 37½in) for bag lining
  2 rectangles, each 36 x 15cm (14 x 6in), for base and lining
  2 rectangles, each 26 x 31.5cm (10¼ x 12½in), for flap and lining
  2 strips, each 15 x 80cm (6 x 31½in), for straps
  1 strip 12 x 2.5cm (4¾ x 1in) for loop
  1 strip 12cm x 1m (4¾ x 39in) for rope casing
- **Wadding/batting**
  1 rectangle 40 x 95cm (15¾ x 37½in)
  1 rectangle 36 x 15cm (14 x 6in)
  1 rectangle 26 x 31.5cm (10¼ x 12½in)
  2 strips, each 7.5 x 80cm (3 x 31½in)

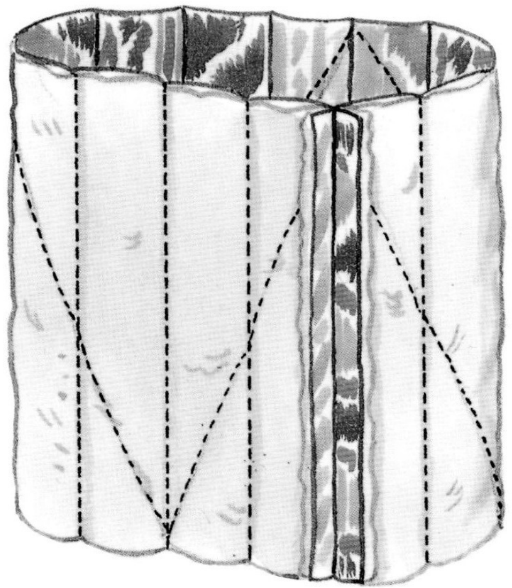

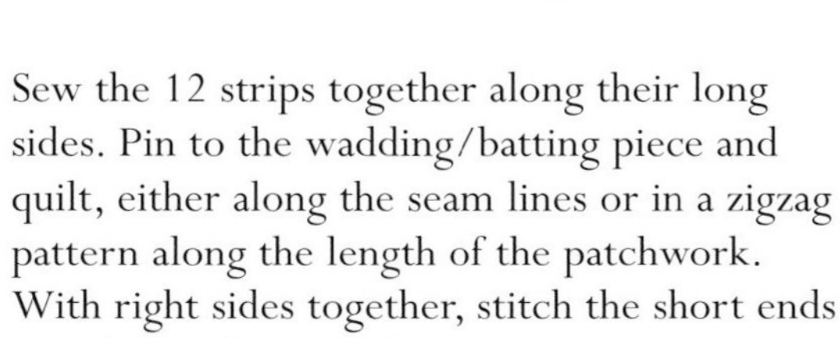

1 Sew the 12 strips together along their long sides. Pin to the wadding/batting piece and quilt, either along the seam lines or in a zigzag pattern along the length of the patchwork. With right sides together, stitch the short ends together to form a tube.

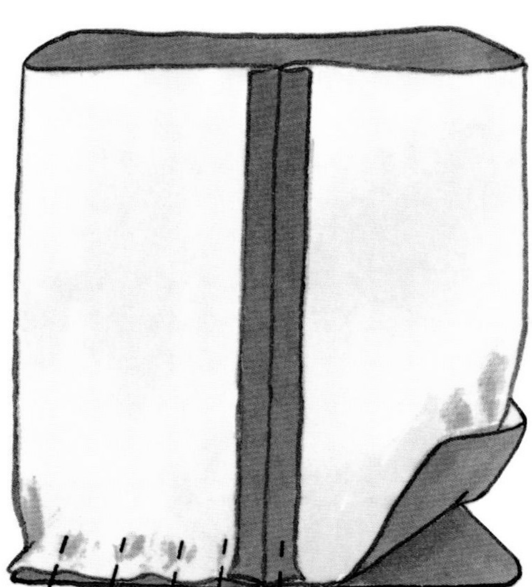

2 With right sides together, stitch together the two short sides of the bag lining. Round the corners of one of the bag bases with scissors and with right sides together, pin to the bag lining. Stitch.

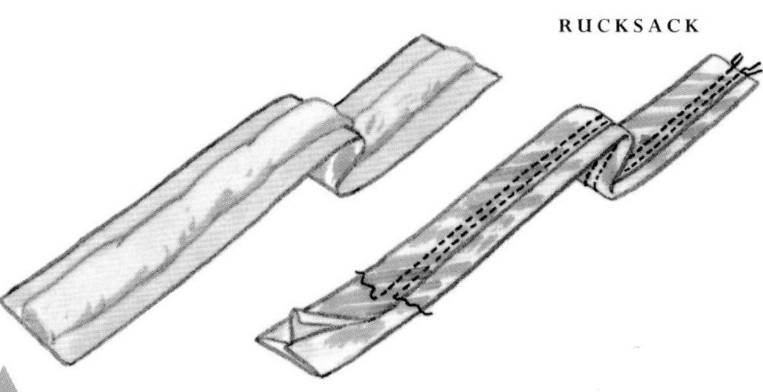

3 Centre one of the wadding strips along one of the strap pieces and fold the fabric around it. Turn under the raw edge of the uppermost fabric and stitch two rows, 6mm ($\frac{1}{4}$in) apart, down the centre of the strap. Repeat for the other strap.

4 Diagonally quilt the remaining bag base to its corresponding wadding/batting piece. Round the corners with scissors. Pin the straps, matching raw edges, to the ends of the right side of the quilted base.

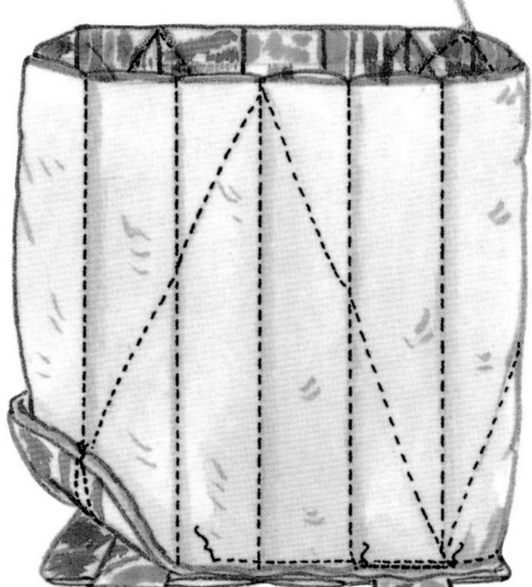

5 With right sides together pin the quilted base to the quilted tube and stitch, backstitching at the straps for extra strength. With right sides outwards, insert the bag lining into the rucksack.

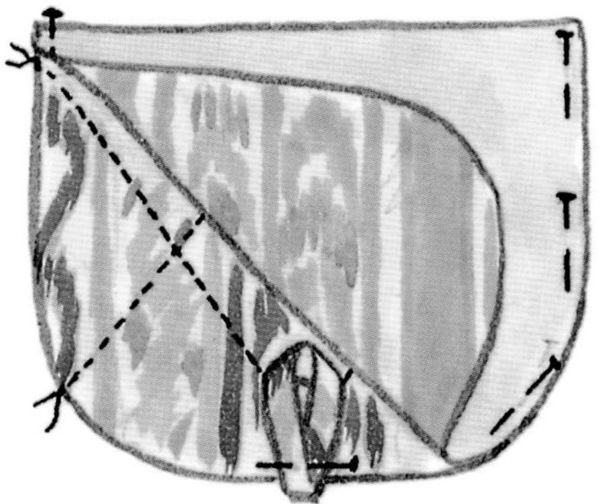

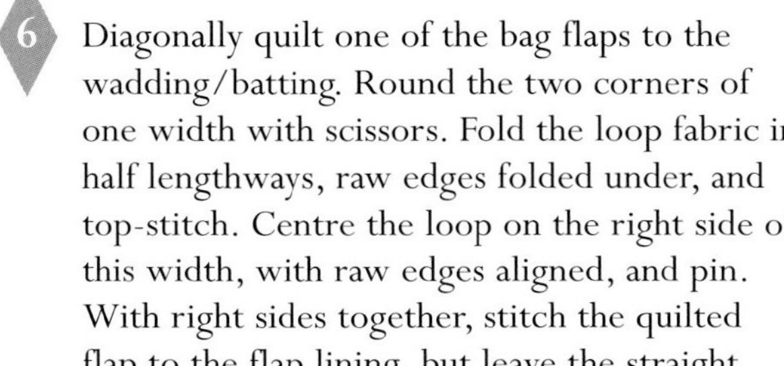

6 Diagonally quilt one of the bag flaps to the wadding/batting. Round the two corners of one width with scissors. Fold the loop fabric in half lengthways, raw edges folded under, and top-stitch. Centre the loop on the right side of this width, with raw edges aligned, and pin. With right sides together, stitch the quilted flap to the flap lining, but leave the straight edge open.

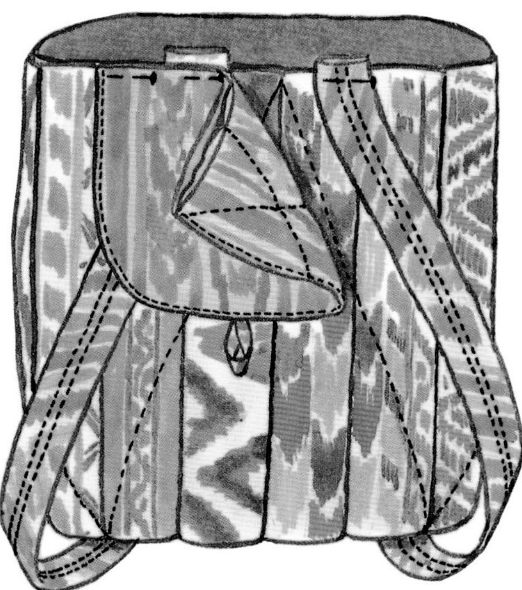

7 Turn the flap right side out and top-stitch 1cm (½in) in from the seam edge. Pin the straps to the top of the rucksack so that they are 8cm (3in) apart. With right sides together, pin the flap to the back of the rucksack, centring it over the straps.

8 Fold the ends of the rope casing to the wrong side. With right sides together, pin the casing to the inside edge of the rucksack top, making sure that the ends meet at the centre front of the bag. Stitch. Fold the casing over to the right side, folding under the raw edge by 1cm (½in), and top-stitch just below the previous stitch line.

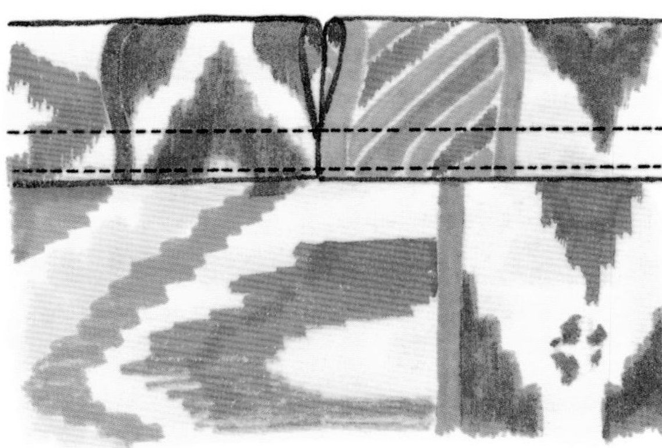

9 To enclose the raw edges of the bag, stitch 1cm (½in) above the lower edge of the casing. Thread the cord through the rope casing and knot the ends. Position the toggle on the rucksack to fit the loop, and hand stitch in place.

Make-up Bag

This brightly coloured bag, reminiscent of a jester's hat, could be made bigger and used as a shoe bag, but a casing would have to be added for the draw-string.

Finished measurements:
32cm (12¾in) high (including cuff), 62cm (24½in) circumference

MATERIALS

- 30cm (12in) plain yellow fabric
- 30cm (12in) plain blue fabric
- 20cm (8in) plain red fabric
- 20cm (8in) plain green fabric
- 30cm (12in) PVC or cotton fabric for lining
- 41cm (16in) wadding/batting
- red or green thread
- 2 large plastic or wooden beads

PREPARATION

Cut the following pieces:

- **Red and green fabrics**
  2 strips, each 60 x 7cm (23½ x 2¾in)
- **Yellow and blue fabrics**
  3 strips, each 60 x 7cm (23½ x 2¾in)
  6 strips, each 11 x 7cm (4¼ x 2¾in)
- **Wadding/batting**
  1 rectangle 62 x 38cm (24½ x 15in)
- **PVC or cotton lining**
  1 rectangle 62 x 22cm (24½ x 8¾in)
  1 circle with a 7.5cm (3in) radius

1 Sew five 60cm (23½in) strips together in this order: yellow, blue, red, green, yellow to form a rectangle. Sew a further five strips in this order to form another rectangle: blue, yellow, green, red, blue.

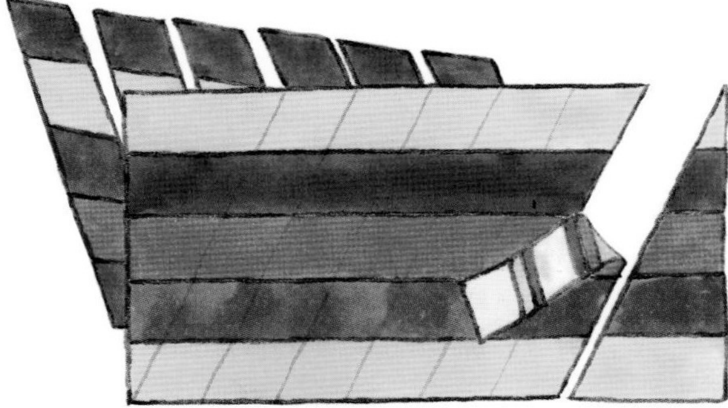

2 Cut six strips out of the first rectangle, each strip 7.5cm (3in) wide and cut at an angle of 60 degrees to the top edge (use your set square if you do not have a protractor). Repeat with the second rectangle, reversing the direction of the angled strips. Save the remaining patchwork for the draw-string.

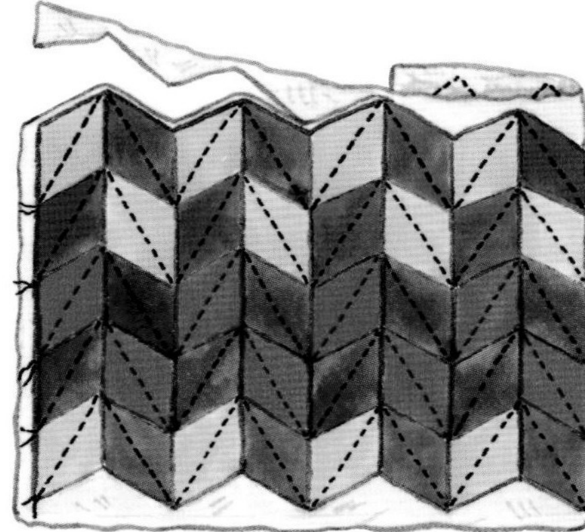

3 Alternate the strips and stitch together. Pin the patchwork to the wadding then quilt across the long diagonals of the chevron rows with a long machine stitch. Trim the wadding.

4 Join the two short edges together to form a tube. The section with the single row of blue and yellow chevrons is the base. With right sides together, join the points to one another so that they meet in the centre. The bag sits on the axes of a six-pointed star.

5 To make the cuff of the bag, stitch the remaining short yellow and blue strips together along the long edges. Join the short ends together to form a tube. With right sides together, pin the cuff to the top of the bag with the top raw edge in line with the uppermost points of the bag. Match the seams. Stitch along the bag edge, then cut the cuff 6mm ($\frac{1}{4}$in) from the seam.

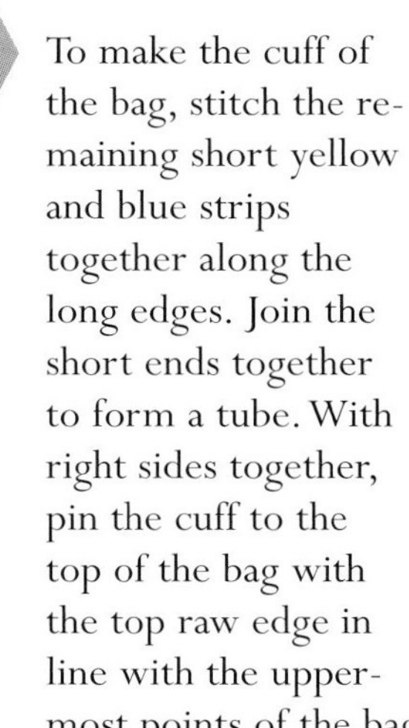

6 Stitch the lining together along the short edges, leaving a 5cm (2in) opening in the middle. With a long machine stitch, work a row of stitches along one end of the tube, then draw up the thread so that the tube fits the base circle. With right sides together, pin the base to the tube, then stitch in place.

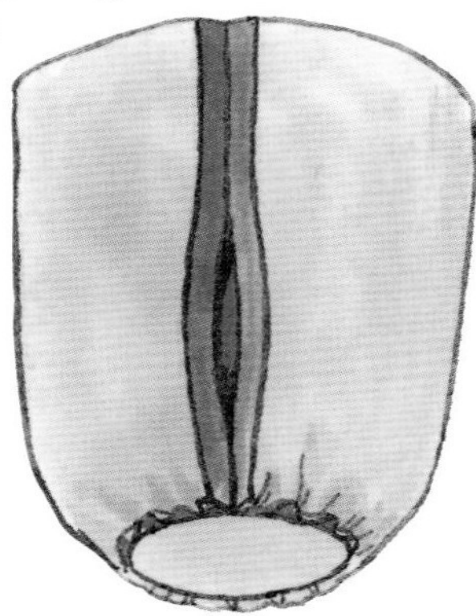

7 With right sides together, stitch the lining to the cuff, then turn the bag to the right side through the opening in the lining. On the outside of the bag, pin, then stitch the bag to the cuff along the lower points of the top row of chevrons. Sew up the opening in the lining.

8 To make the draw-string, cut strips 4cm ($1\frac{1}{2}$in) wide and at an angle of 60 degrees from the remaining patchwork. Stitch together to make a piece 1m (about 40in) long. Press the raw edges to the wrong side, fold in half and top-stitch. Secure to the bag with two vertical rows of stitches at the line where the bag is stitched to the cuff. If wished, finish the ends with wooden beads, held in place by knotting the ends.

WAISTCOAT

The materials given are sufficient for a small to medium adult waistcoat. For a large size, increase the number of diamonds by one in each row. For the basic waistcoat pattern, use one of the commercially prepared paper patterns, or make up your own.

Finished measurements:
back length of small waistcoat 57cm (22½in); to fit bust 87–92cm (34–36in)

MATERIALS

- diamond template
- 20cm (8in) turquoise dupion silk
- 20cm (8in) green dupion silk
- 20cm (8in) fuchsia dupion silk
- 20cm (8in) deep red dupion silk
- 80cm (32in) black dupion silk
- 80cm (32in) black lining fabric
- 6 self-covering buttons, 15mm (about ¾in) diameter
- 80cm (32in) interfacing
- black thread
- waistcoat pattern pieces

PREPARATION

Cut the following pieces:

- **Turquoise, green, red and pink silks**
  20 diamonds from each, cut using the template
- **Turquoise silk**
  2 belts
- **Lining fabric**
  2 waistcoat fronts and 1 back
- **Black silk**
  1 waistcoat back
  cover the buttons following the manufacturer's instructions
- **Interfacing**
  2 front pieces

Template actual size

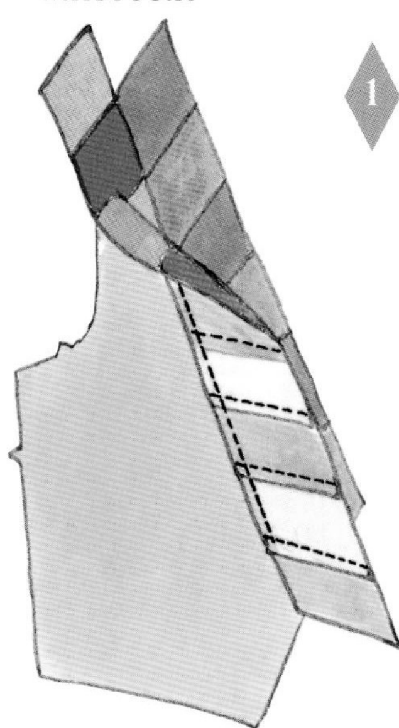

1 Alternate three green and three pink diamonds in a row along the length of the waistcoat front pattern, following the neck line. Sew the diamonds together so that they are in the same position on the pattern. Make sure that when the diamonds are sewn together, the points are offset by the seam allowance.

2 Repeat step 1, alternating rows of red and turquoise diamonds with rows of pink and green diamonds. You will need 6 rows in all for each waistcoat front, arranged as shown in the illustration. Join the rows together, then pin the pattern to the right side of the patchwork. Cut out.

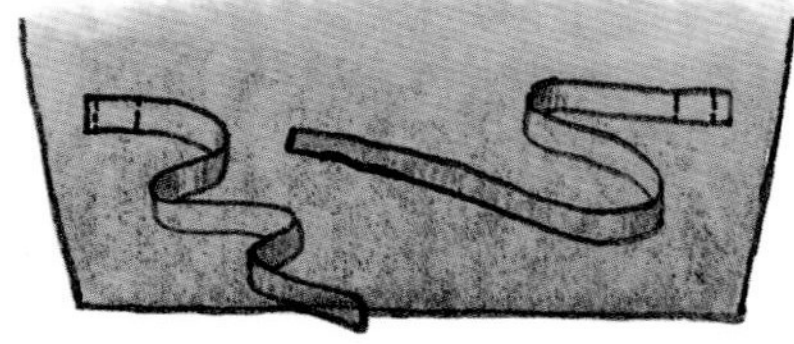

3 Repeat steps 1 and 2, this time with the pattern wrong side up to complete the other side. Fold the belt sections in half lengthways, right sides together, and stitch along the long edge and one short edge. Turn to the right side and press. Pin the belts to the outside of the waistcoat back, matching dots. Stitch along the seam lines.

4 Machine baste the interfacing to the wrong side of the waistcoat fronts. With right sides together, stitch the waistcoat fronts to the back at shoulders. Stitch the lining fronts to the lining back at shoulders.

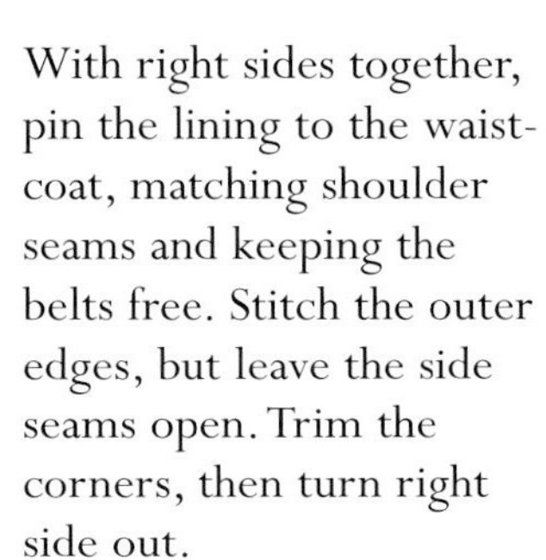

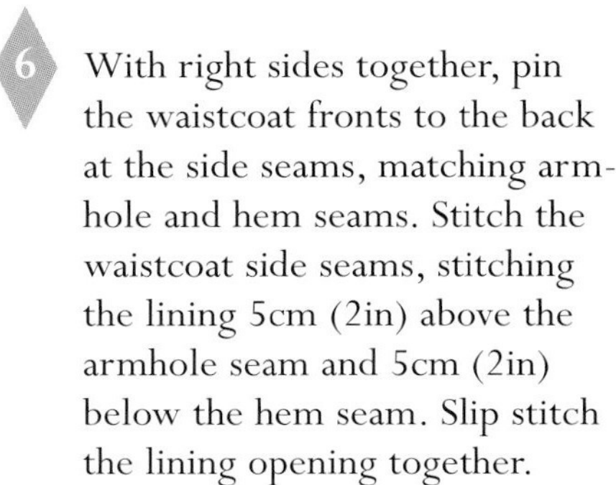

5 With right sides together, pin the lining to the waistcoat, matching shoulder seams and keeping the belts free. Stitch the outer edges, but leave the side seams open. Trim the corners, then turn right side out.

6 With right sides together, pin the waistcoat fronts to the back at the side seams, matching armhole and hem seams. Stitch the waistcoat side seams, stitching the lining 5cm (2in) above the armhole seam and 5cm (2in) below the hem seam. Slip stitch the lining opening together.

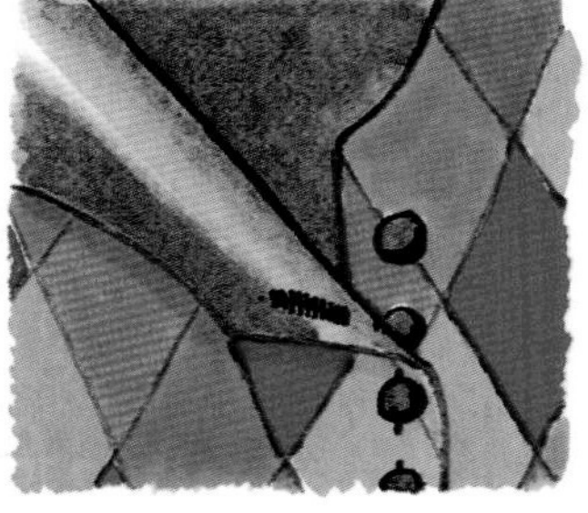

7 Make six evenly spaced buttonholes on the right front of the waistcoat about 15mm (¾in) in from the edge. Lap the right front over the left and sew six buttons under the buttonholes. (For a man's waistcoat, reverse.)

SLEEVELESS JACKET

This unisex jacket is approximately a woman's UK size 14 (US size 12) or a man's medium size. For UK size 12 (US size 10), cut the horizontal pieced strips into four panels, each 16cm (6¼in) wide; for UK size 10 (US size 8), cut four panels, each 14cm (5½in) wide. The size can be altered by adding or eliminating strips. Pin it on before quilting to check and adjust the size as necessary.

To make a child's jacket to go with the patchwork skirt (see pages 44–7), cut the 13 horizontal pieced strips into four panels, each 11.5cm (4½in) wide, with each strip 4cm (1½in) wide. The side panels are two-thirds of the length of the pieced strips. Make the centre and side flared panels 3cm (1¼in) wide at the top and 6cm (2½in) wide at the bottom.

Finished measurements:
chest 120cm (47in), back length 75cm (approximately 29in)

MATERIALS

- 2.5m (2½yd) navy and red striped fabric
- 2 checked shirts (one red and one green)
- 150cm (60in) wadding/batting
- 1m (1yd) navy needlecord
- 6 snap fasteners
- blue thread

PREPARATION

Cut or rip the following pieces:

- **Navy and red fabric**
  7 strips, each 7 x 76cm (2¾ x 30in), along the length for the horizontal strip panels
  1 strip 12 x 70cm (4¾ x 27½in) for the centre-back
  2 strips, each 7 x 46cm (2¾ x 18in), for the sides
  2 strips, each 7 x 70cm (2¾ x 27½in), for the front overlaps
  2 strips, each 5 x 22cm (2 x 8½in), for tops of front panels
  1 strip 5 x 49cm (2 x 19¼in) for top of back
  1 strip 7 x 64cm (2¾ x 25¼in) for collar
  2 strips, each 3.5 x 16cm (1¼ x 6¼in), to cover the shoulder seams
  2 strips, each 7cm (2¾in) wide, cut across the width, which, when sewn together, give a total length of 150cm (60in)
  1 piece, 1.5m (1½yd) long, cut in half across the width and stitched along the length, for the lining
- **Red shirt**
  3 strips, each 5.5 x 76cm (2¼ x 30in), for the horizontal strip panels
  1 strip 7 x 64cm (2¾ x 25¼in) for the collar lining
- **Green shirt**
  3 strips, each 5.5 x 76cm (2¼ x 30in)
  4 strips, each 6 x 46cm (2½ x 30in)
- **Blue needlecord**
  Strips 4cm (1½in) wide, ripped along the grain; you will need approximately 11 strips, but cut the length to fit as you sew

back of neck
centre back
front of neck

Neck opening pattern actual size

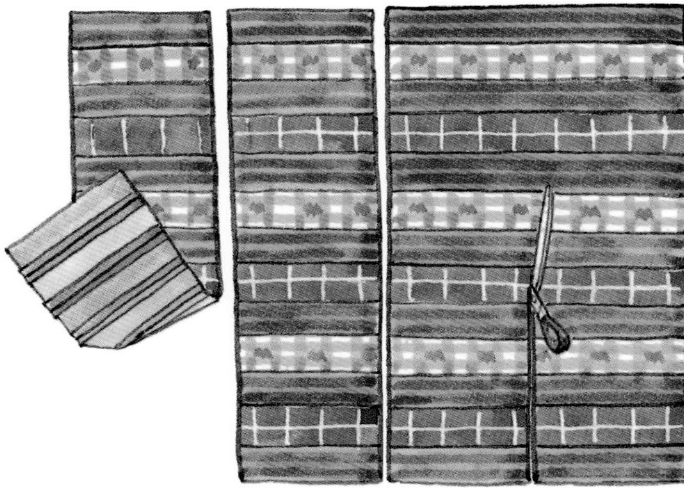

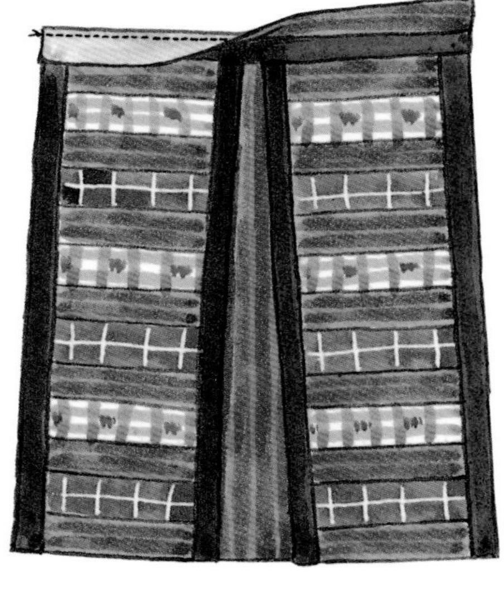

1 Sew the 13 76cm (30in) strips together, alternating the navy stripe fabric with the shirts, starting and ending with the navy stripe. Cut the rectangle into four equal panels across the strips.

4 Stitch the two pieced panels on each side of the flared panel (making sure pieced panels match). Stitch a needlecord strip across the top and trim, then attach the 5 x 49cm (2 x 19¼in) navy stripe strip along the top edge.

2 For the back, sew a needlecord strip along both long edges of two pieced panels. Trim the cord to the correct length.

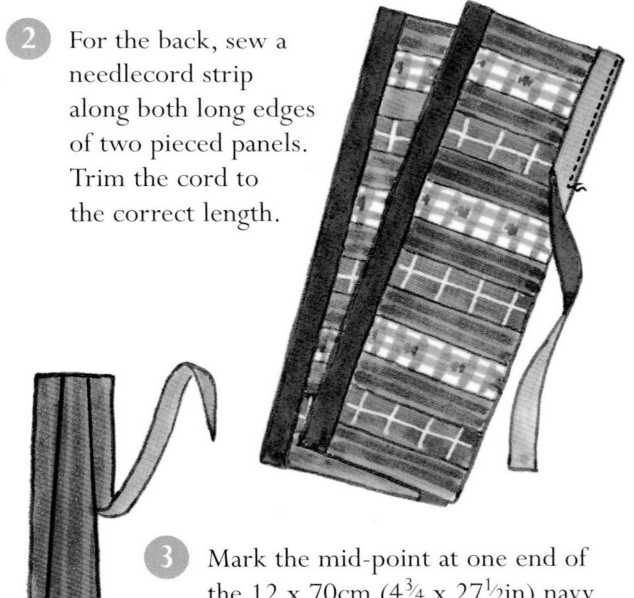

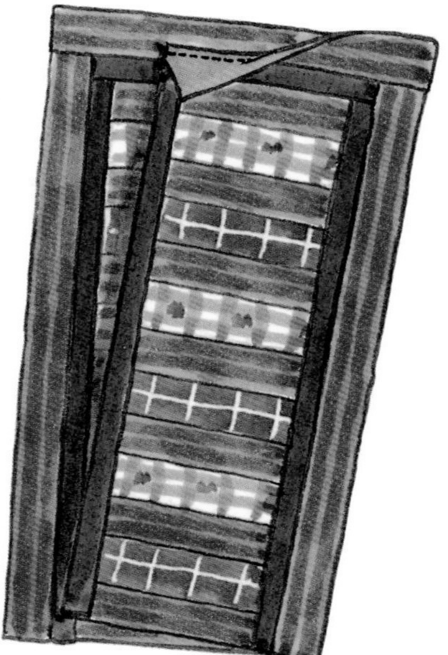

3 Mark the mid-point at one end of the 12 x 70cm (4¾ x 27½in) navy stripe, centre-back strip, mark a point 2cm (¾in) each side of this point. With a long ruler draw a line from these two points to the outer corners at the other end of the strip. Cut along these lines to make a flared panel.

5 For the front, sew a blue cord strip along both long edges of one of the remaining pieced panels, then a needlecord strip across the top. Stitch a 7 x 70cm (2¾ x 27½in) navy stripe strip along one length of the panel, then stitch a 5 x 29cm (2 x 11½in) navy stripe strip across the top. Repeat with the other panel.

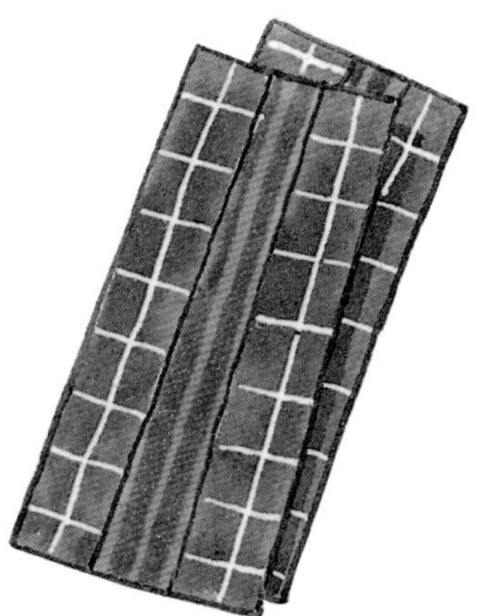

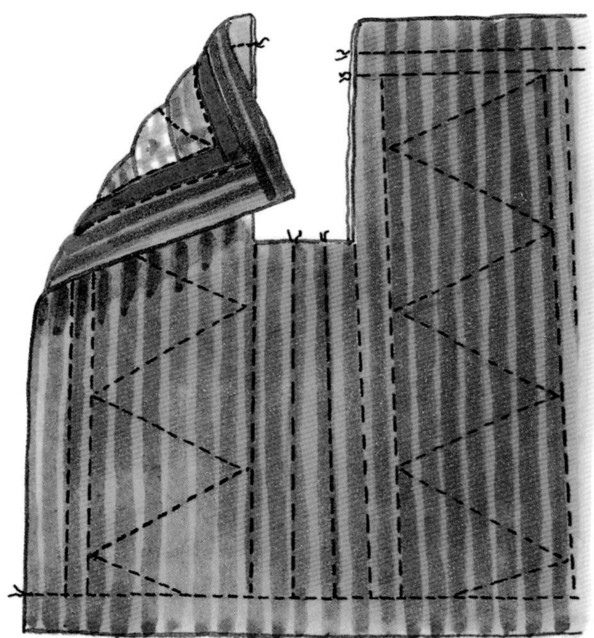

6 For the side, make a flared panel in the same way as for the back out of a navy stripe 7 x 46cm ($2^{3}/4$ x 18in) strip, but tapering to 4cm ($1^{1}/2$in) at the top. Stitch green checked strips on each of the long edges. Repeat for the other side section.

7 Join the side panels to the back, then the fronts to the sides. If desired, sew a needlecord strip across the bottom; this will increase the length of the jacket by 2.5cm (1in). Sew the 150 x 7cm (60 x $2^{3}/4$in) navy strip with vertical stripes around the bottom edge.

8 Lay the wadding/batting on top of the wrong side of the lining fabric. Pin the jacket to the wadding/batting and the lining, and cut it out. Quilt with a long machine stitch in a zigzag pattern across the pieced sections, then along the seam lines of the rest of the jacket. Trim.

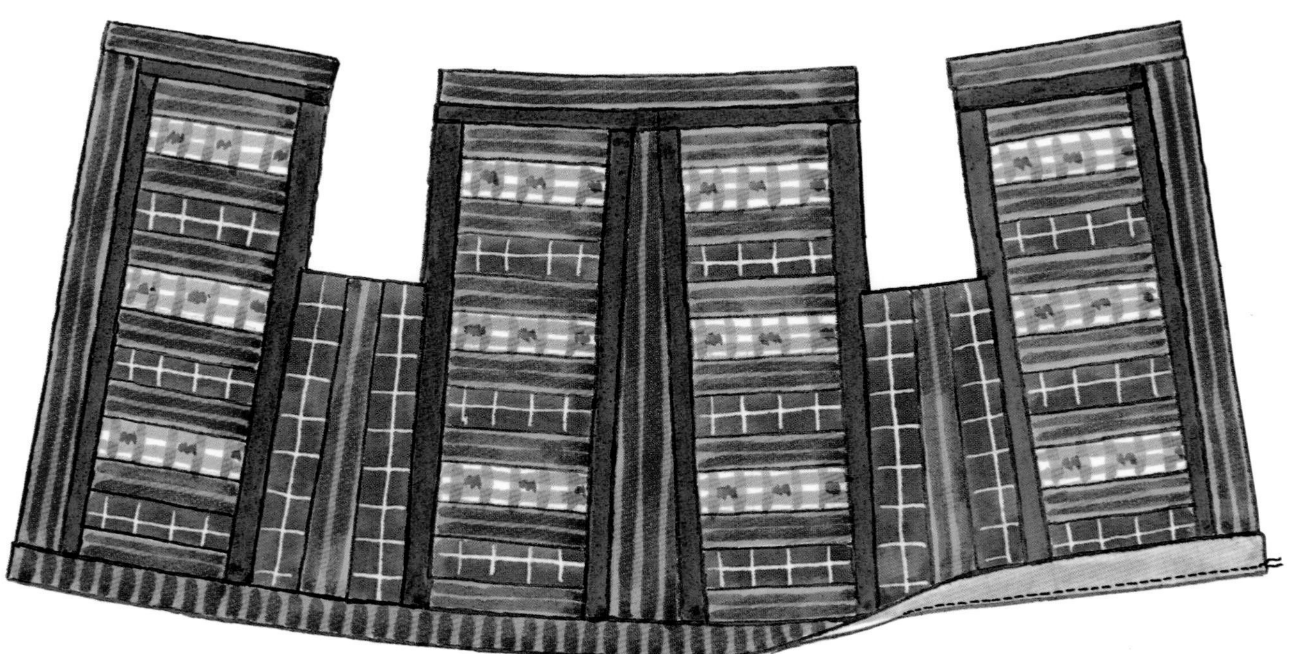

9 With linings together, sew the front to the back at shoulders, starting 20cm (8in) from the armhole. Angle the seam from 1.5cm (just over ½in) to 4.5cm (1¾in) from the needlecord strip. Trim the seam.

10 Pin the neck opening pattern (see page 39) to the centre of the back and cut along the back-neck line. Pin the pattern to the centre of the overlapping front sections, taking care that the patchwork is aligned, and cut along the front-neck line.

11 Cover the raw edges of the shoulder seams with the 3.5 x 16cm (1¼ x 6¼in) navy stripe strips, folding under the raw edges of the long edges and top-stitching in place. Bind the front raw edges with needlecord, then bind the bottom edge of the jacket and, finally, the armholes, starting at the base of the armhole.

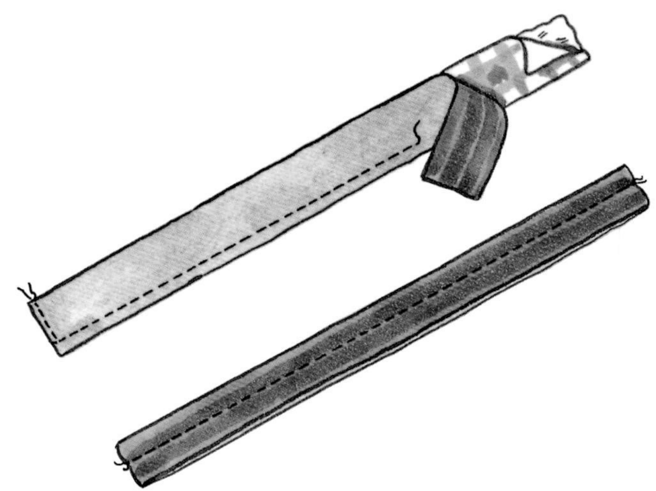

12 Cut a piece of wadding/batting to fit the collar piece. With right sides together, stitch the navy stripe collar fabric to the checked collar lining and wadding along the two short edges and along one long edge. Turn the right way out, and quilt along the centre line.

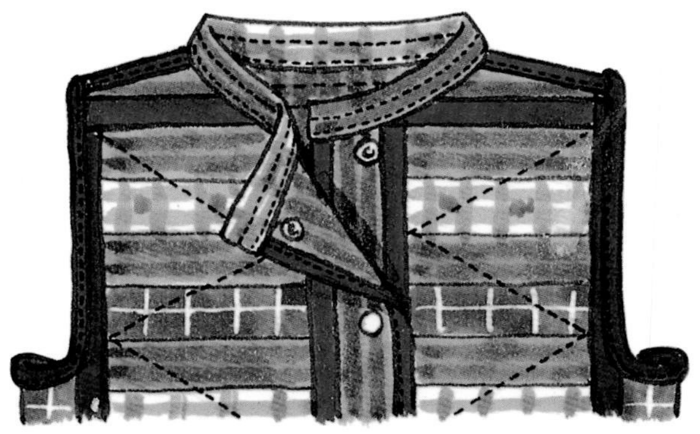

13 Pin, then stitch the collar lining to the inside of the jacket. Fold the right side of the collar over the seam. Fold under the raw edge and top-stitch in place. Overlap the front (right over left for women; left over right for men) so that the binding is level with the first blue strip and attach the snap fasteners to the front of the jacket, following the manufacturer's instructions and spacing them evenly.

Child's Skirt

This makes a skirt for an eight- or nine-year-old. For a younger or older girl, reduce or increase the number of lower bands to change the length. To modify the fullness, increase or decrease the length of the horizontal strips. Adjust the lining accordingly.

Finished measurements:
60cm (23½in) long, 56cm (22in) waist, 158cm (62in) bottom edge

MATERIALS

- 10cm (4in) each of five different plum-coloured floral/geometric fabrics
- 10cm (4in) cerise-coloured floral fabric
- 1m (1yd) airforce blue needlecord
- 1m (1yd) bottle green needlecord
- 1m (1yd) dark red needlecord
- 1m (1yd) plum needlecord
- 150cm (60in) black lining fabric
- 60cm (24in) buttonhole elastic or plain elastic, 1cm (½in) wide
- 1 button (if using buttonhole elastic)
- black thread

PREPARATION

Cut or rip the following pieces:

- **Plum fabrics**
  1 strip 5 x 90cm (2 x 35½in) from each fabric; choose 2 of the fabrics and repeat to give 7 strips in all, for horizontal strip panels

  1 piece from 1 colour, 5 x 76cm (2 x 30in), for waistband lining
- **Cerise fabric**
  2 strips, each 5 x 90cm (2 x 35½in), for horizontal strip panels
- **Blue and green needlecord**
  2 strips, each 4 x 90cm (1½ x 35½in), for horizontal strip panels
- **Blue, plum, green and red needlecord**
  7 strips, each 4 x 50cm (1½ x 19¾in), for vertical strip panels

  2 strips, each 4cm x 1m (1½ x 39in); stitch the 2 strips together across the width to give a 2m (78in) length in each colour to go round bottom of skirt
- **Plum needlecord**
  1 strip 5 x 76cm (2 x 30in) for waistband
- **Lining fabric**
  2 pieces, cut across the width and stitched together to give a piece 2m x 60cm (78 x 23½in)

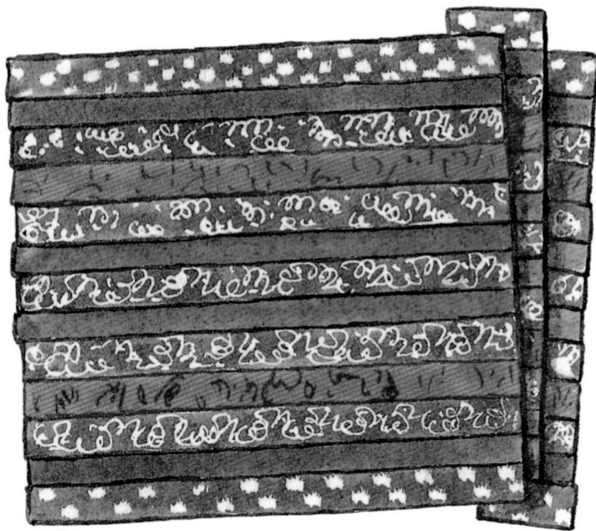

1 Alternate the plum fabrics with the blue and green needlecords and cerise fabric and stitch together along the long edges. Cut into seven panels, each 12½cm (5in) wide.

2 Stitch red, green, plum and blue 50cm (19¾in) needlecord strips together to make seven panels, each of four colours. Alternate these with the vertical patchwork panels and stitch together. Trim the patchwork along the top and bottom to even the edges.

3 Sew the long red, green, plum and blue strips along the bottom length of the patchwork. Trim the strips to fit. Sew the patchwork to the lining along the lower edge (where the hem will be). Open out and press. Trim the lining. Fold in half widthways, matching raw edges and seams. Pin and stitch along the short edges of the lining and patchwork.

4 Turn right side out and turn the lining to the inside of the skirt. Carefully press, turning the patchwork under by 6mm (¼in) along the bottom edge. Pin the lining to the patchwork along the top.

5 Machine baste two rows 6mm ($^{1}/_{4}$in) and 15mm (about $^{3}/_{4}$in) from the top. Pull up the threads and gather the skirt to 5cm (2in) more than the hip measurements.

6 Stitch the waistband to the waistband lining along one long edge. Bring the waistband ends together, right sides together, and stitch the waistband as far as the waistband lining, then backstitch to the beginning. Fold over to the right side. Top stitch with long machine stitch, 6mm ($^{1}/_{4}$in) from the fold.

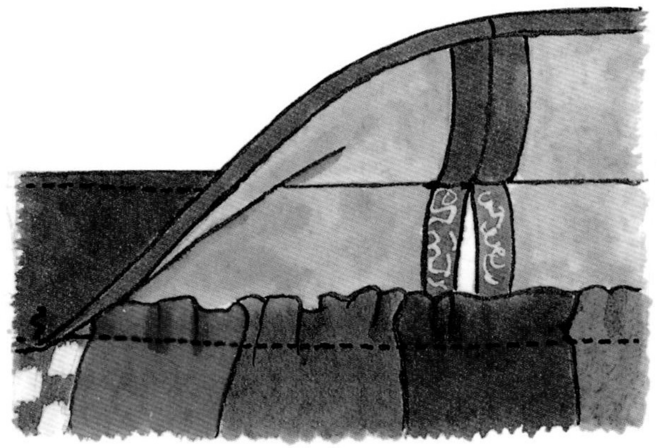

7 With right sides together, sew the waistband lining to the inside of the skirt, matching raw edges. Fold the waistband over to the right side. Fold under the raw edge by 6mm ($^{1}/_{4}$in) and top-stitch, just below previous seam line.

8 Measure the waist and cut the elastic accordingly, allowing 5cm (2in) extra. Insert in the opening in the waistband lining. Secure one end of the elastic with a button sewn on top of waistband lining and through the elastic inside the waistband and pull up the buttonholes in the other end of the elastic to fit. Alternatively, simply insert normal elastic, draw up to fit and slip stitch the opening closed.

LITTLE PURSE

This purse, which uses the quilt-as-you-go method, is very quick and easy to make.

Finished measurements: 10.5 x 15cm (4 x 6in), with a 106cm (42in) strap

MATERIALS

- 9 strips, each 4 x 15cm ($1\frac{3}{4}$ x 6in), in a variety of fabrics
- 15 x 30cm (6 x 12in) contrasting fabric for lining
- 15 x 30cm (6 x 12in) wadding/batting
- 3 x 150cm ($1\frac{1}{4}$ x 60in) needlecord in a complimentary colour for binding
- matching thread
- 1 popper

1 Pin or baste the wadding/batting to the wrong side of the lining. Lay the first strip, right side up, on top of the wadding, with the raw edges aligned. Place a second strip on top of the first, right sides together. Pin and stitch.

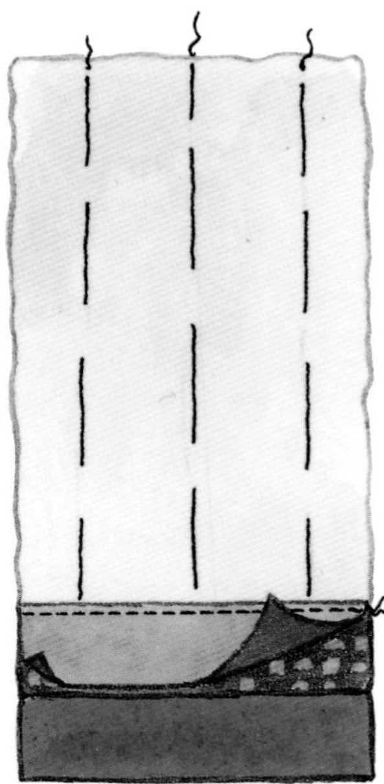

2 Fold the second strip so it is right side up, and finger press. Repeat until all strips are used. Press.

3 Trim so that the patchwork measures 15 x 25cm (6 x 10in). Sew 15cm (6in) of binding strip to the wrong side of one short end. Fold the binding over to the right side, turn under the long raw edge and top-stitch. Curve the corners of the other end.

4 Fold the bound edge to the wrong side to make a pocket about 9cm (3½in) deep. Pin in place. Starting at the bottom of the purse, bind the raw edges as before, tucking under the ends of the binding before stitching. Ease the binding around the curves.

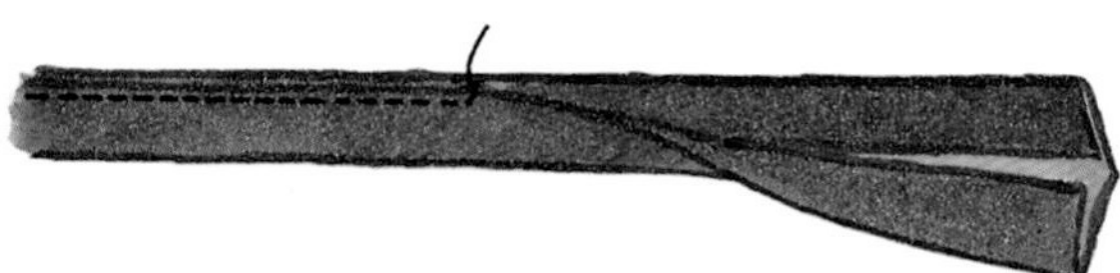

5 To make the strap, press the raw edges of the remaining binding to the wrong side so that they meet in the centre, then fold over and top-stitch.

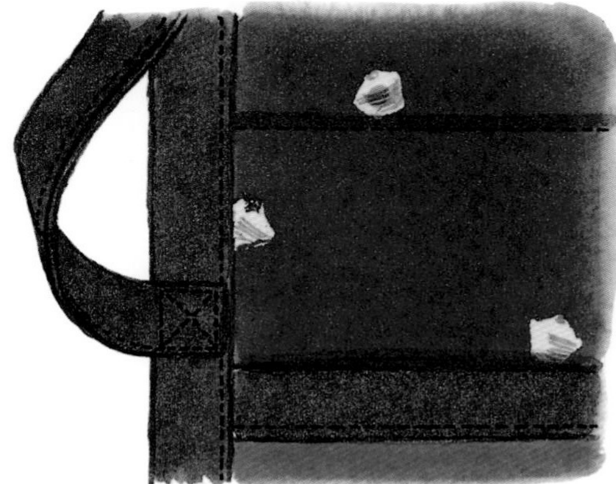

6 Folding under the raw edges of the strap ends, pin the strap to the inside of the purse just below the flap fold. Secure by stitching a cross in a square. Attach a popper to the centre of the flap and purse, following the manufacturer's instructions.

Scrunchy

You can use strips of varying widths for this scrunchy or you could try cutting the pieced strips on the diagonal, to produce a slanted stripe. For evenings, use velvets, satins or silks and make the strips longer to give a fuller, more sophisticated look.

MATERIALS

- 3 strips of fabric, each 39 x 5cm (15 x 2in)
- 18cm (7in) elastic
- matching thread

Stitch the strips together along the long edges, then cut into three equal sections. Join the sections together to form a piece 45cm (18in) long.

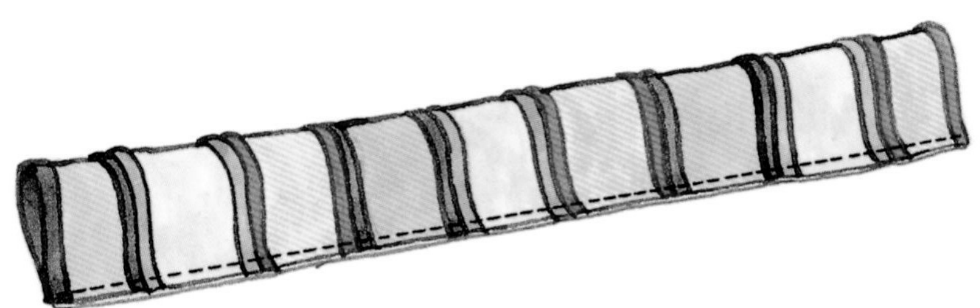

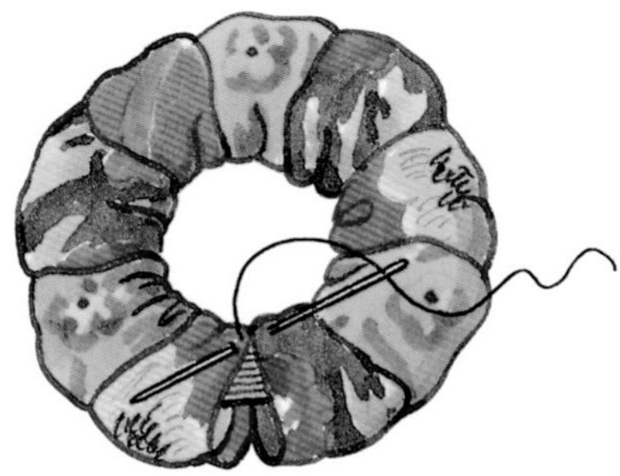

Press the seams open and press the raw edges of the ends to the wrong side. Fold the rectangle in half lengthways and stitch.

Turn the tube right side out. Insert the elastic and stitch by hand to secure. Slip stitch the ends of the scrunchy together.

HAIRBAND

The hairband is made in much the same way as the Scrunchy (see opposite page).

MATERIALS

- 6 strips of fabric, each 39 x 5cm (15 x 2in)
- 45cm (18in) elastic (enough to go around head plus 5cm/2in)
- matching thread

1 Stitch the strips together, then cut the resulting rectangle into three equal sections. Join the sections together to form a rectangle 90 x 13cm (36 x 5in).

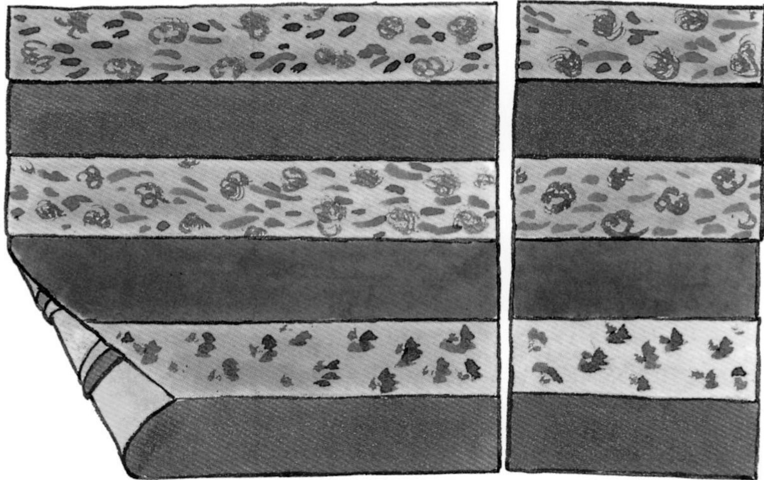

2 Press the seams open and press the raw edges of the ends to the wrong side. Fold in half lengthways and stitch.

3 Turn right side out. Press, with the seam running along the centre of the tube, then stitch two rows, 2cm ($\frac{3}{4}$in) apart, on either side of the centre seam, using a long machine stitch.

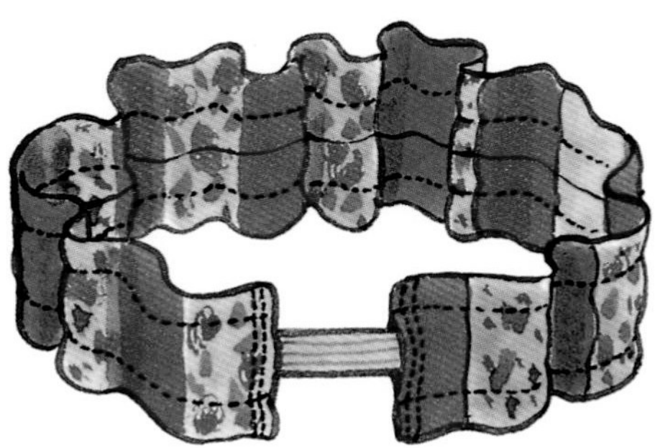

4 Insert the elastic down the centre of the hairband, leaving 2.5cm (1in) of elastic exposed at each end. Tuck the elastic into the opposite ends of the hairband. Pin. Machine stitch the ends of the hairband forwards and backwards to secure the elastic and enclose the raw edges.

Little House Picture

A variation on the traditional Little Schoolhouse motif, this patchwork picture was inspired by a sampler stitched in the middle of the nineteenth century.

Finished measurements:
23 x 25.5cm (9 x 10in)

MATERIALS

- 1 roof template
- 20cm (8in) blue and cream floral fabric
- 30cm (12in) dark pink fabric
- 5cm (2in) beige check fabric
- 25cm (10in) cream fabric with small pattern
- 30cm (12in) calico
- 30cm (12in) stiff interfacing
- carmine and cream-coloured threads

PREPARATION

Cut the following pieces:

- **Blue and cream floral fabric**
  1 rectangle 16 x 12cm (6¼ x 4¾in) for house
  2 rectangles, each 8 x 3cm (3¼ x 1⅛in), for chimneys
- **Dark pink fabric**
  1 rectangle 18 x 5.5cm (7 x 2¼in), cut out roof shape using template
  1 rectangle 3.25 x 5.5cm (1¼ x 2¼in) for door
  1 rectangle 25 x 28cm (10 x 11in) for background
- **Beige check fabric**
  5 rectangles, each 3.25 x 4.5cm (1¼ x 1¾in), for windows
- **Cream fabric with small pattern**
  1 rectangle 20 x 22.5cm (8 x 8¾in) for background
- **Calico**
  1 rectangle 25 x 28cm (10 x 11in) for backing
  3 rectangles, each 4 x 10cm (1½ x 4in), for loops
- **Stiff interfacing**
  1 rectangle 25 x 28cm (10 x 11in) for backing

Template
actual size

Press the raw edges of the roof sides to the wrong side. With right sides together, pin the house to the roof.

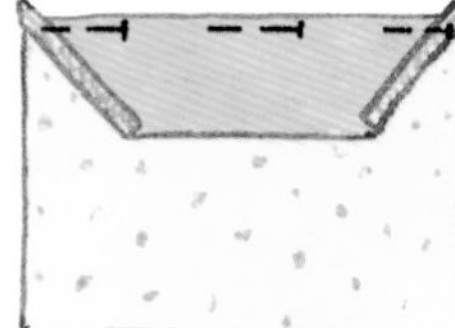

Press the raw edges of one long and one short side of both chimneys to the wrong side. Pin to each side of the roof, with the raw edges of the chimneys aligned with the house. Stitch the roof and chimneys to the house.

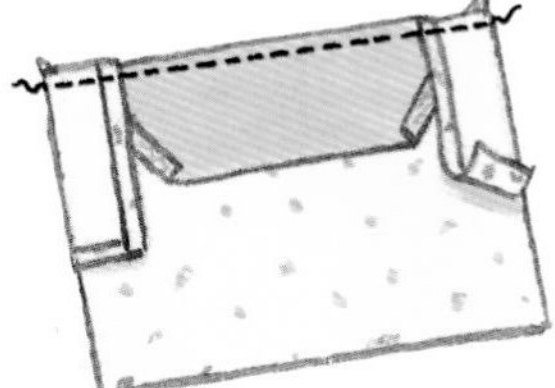

Press the raw edges of the windows and door to the wrong side. Position them on the house, spacing them evenly, then pin and top-stitch along the edges, using carmine thread. Stitch the window panes in carmine thread.

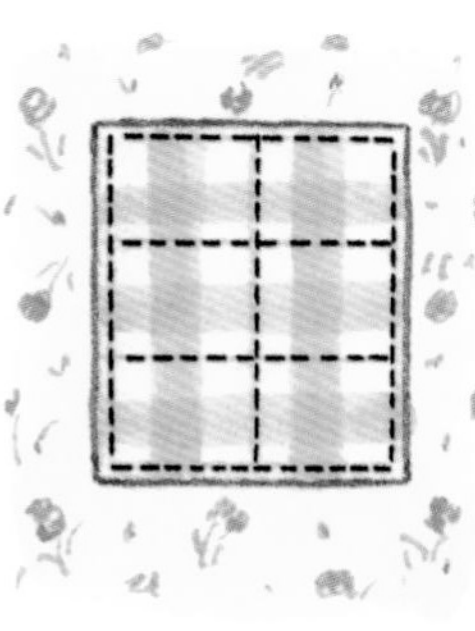

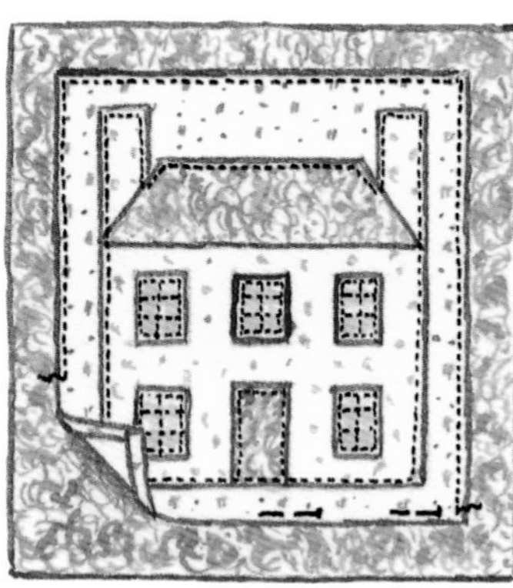

Press under the raw edges of the house, roof and chimneys. Centre the house on the background fabric and pin in place. Top-stitch close to the edges, using carmine thread. Press under the raw edges of the cream-coloured background and centre it on the dark pink background fabric. Top-stitch in place.

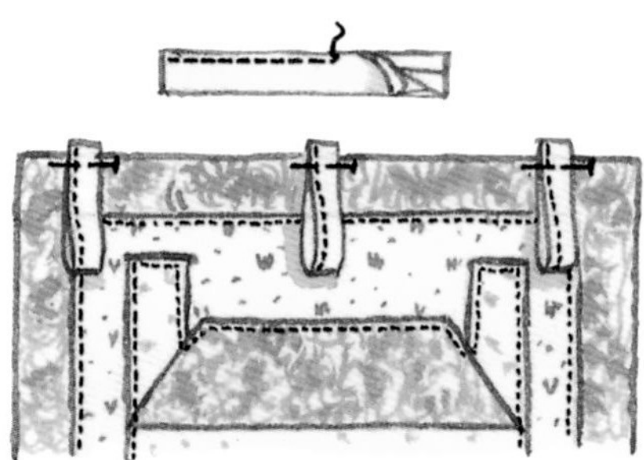

Fold the loops in half lengthways. Turn under the long raw edges and top-stitch. Fold the loops in half and pin to the right side of the pink background, matching the raw edges.

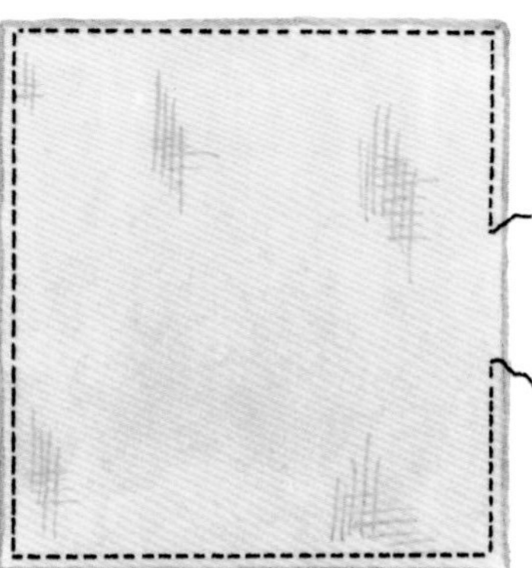

Lay the calico backing on top of the house, then place the interfacing on top. Pin and sew around the edges, leaving a gap of about 9cm ($3\frac{1}{2}$in) along one side.

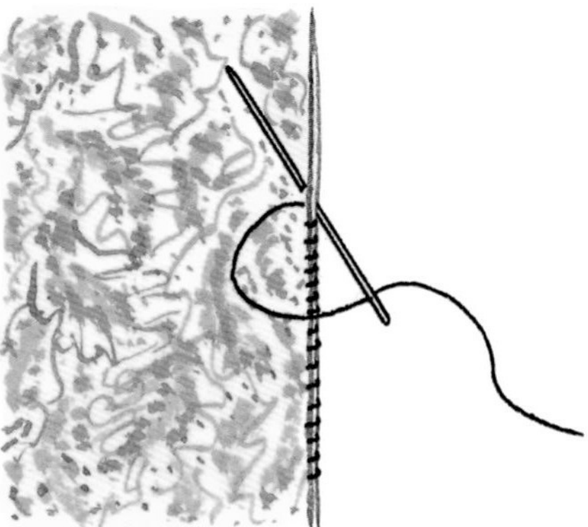

Turn to right side. Press and invisibly close the gap by hand. Hang the picture on a short length of wooden dowel.

TEA COSY

The tea cosy design has seven hexagons separated by white triangles to produce a star motif. The blanketing gives it extra insulation.

Finished measurements: 33 x 25.5cm (13 x 10in)

MATERIALS

- 1 tea cosy template
- 1 9cm ($3\frac{1}{2}$in) equilateral triangle template (see Techniques section for making templates)
- 20cm (8in) fabric in three different red/cerise floral fabrics
- 20cm (8in) fabric in three different blue floral fabrics
- 20cm (8in) sparsely sprigged or plain white fabric
- 41cm (16in) wadding/batting
- 41cm (16in) woollen blanketing for lining
- 12cm ($4\frac{3}{4}$in) blue or red fabric, 2.5cm (1in) wide, for loop
- cerise or blue thread

PREPARATION

Cut the following pieces:

- **Red/cerise fabrics**
  14 triangles from each
- **Blue fabrics**
  14 triangles from each
- **White fabric**
  22 triangles
- **Wadding/batting**
  2 tea cosy shapes
- **Blanketing**
  2 tea cosy shapes

Increase the template on a photocopier until the base is 35cm ($13\frac{3}{4}$in) long before cutting out the patchwork, wadding/batting and blanketing.

Template
enlarge by 400%

Lay one patchwork cosy on top of one wadding/batting piece and quilt along the seam lines of the hexagons. Trim the wadding/batting. Repeat with the other cosy and the other wadding/batting piece.

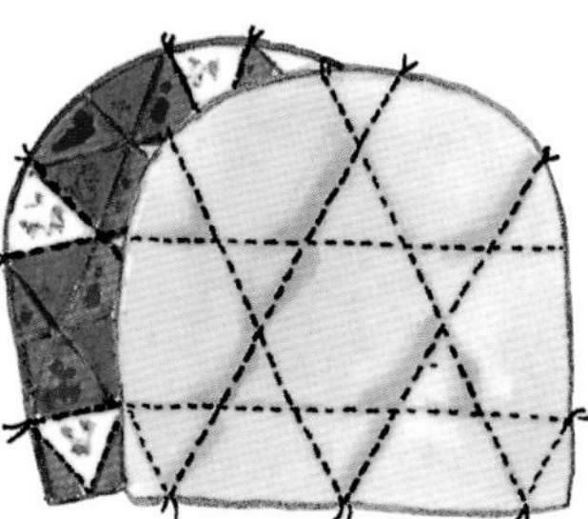

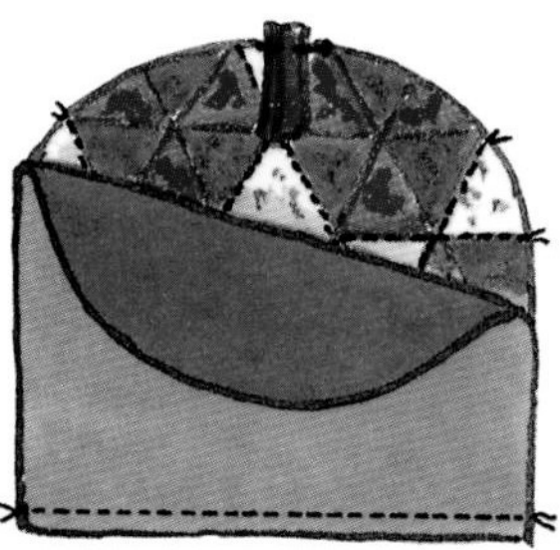

With right sides together, sew one patchwork cosy to one of the lining pieces along the straight edge. Repeat with the other cosy and lining piece. Press the long raw edges of the loop strip to the wrong side. Fold in half, with wrong sides together, and top-stitch. Pin, then tack the loop to the centre of one of the cosy pieces, matching the raw edges. With right sides together, pin the cosies together, matching the seams where the lining is joined to the patchwork. Leaving a 6cm ($2\frac{1}{2}$in) gap in the centre of the lining, machine stitch around the raw edges.

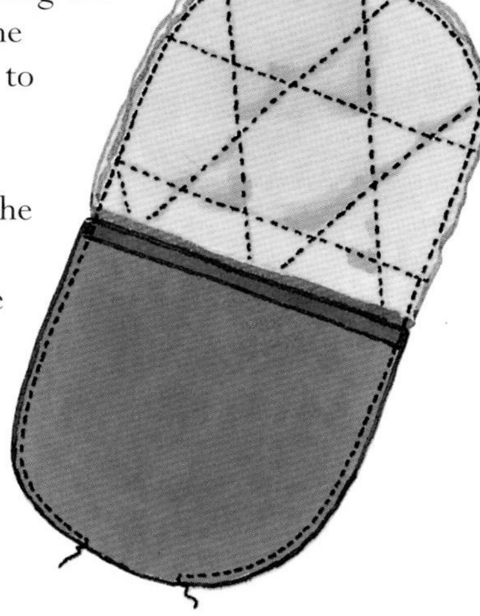

1 Stitch the triangles together in rows, arranging them as indicated. Join the rows together as illustrated.

Using the pattern, cut two cosy shapes from the patchwork, one layer at a time.

Turn to the right side through the gap in the lining. Slip stitch the lining closed. Push the lining to the inside of the cosy.

EGG COSY

The egg cosy is made in the same way as the tea cosy, but using a smaller template. The materials listed here are sufficient to make one egg cosy.

Finished measurements:
11.5 x 14cm ($4\frac{1}{2}$ x $5\frac{1}{2}$in)

MATERIALS

- 1 egg cosy template
- 1 6cm ($2\frac{1}{2}$in) equilateral triangle template (see Techniques section for making templates)
- 6cm ($2\frac{1}{4}$in) wide strip blue and white floral fabric
- 6cm ($2\frac{1}{4}$in) wide strip blue checked fabric
- 20cm (8in) blue on white ticking
- 20cm (8in) wadding
- pale blue thread

PREPARATION

Cut the following pieces:

- **Blue and white floral fabric**
  22 triangles
  1 strip 2.5 x 12cm (1 x $4\frac{1}{2}$in) for the loop
- **Blue checked fabric**
  18 triangles
- **Ticking**
  12 triangles
  2 egg cosy shapes for the lining, using the template
- **Wadding/batting**
  2 egg cosy shapes, using the template.

Increase the template on a photocopier until the base is 13.5cm ($5\frac{1}{4}$in) long before cutting out the patchwork and wadding.

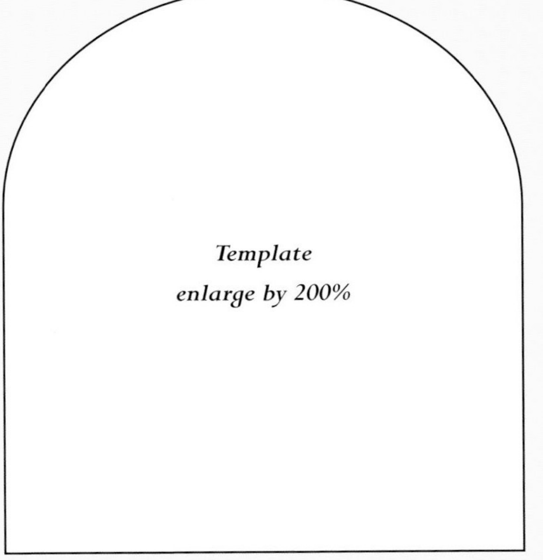

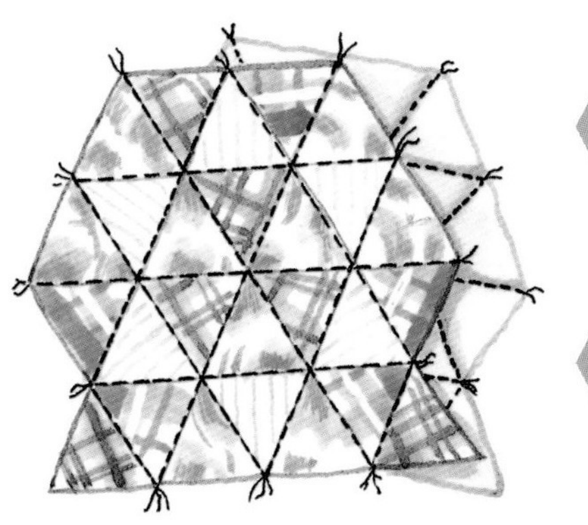

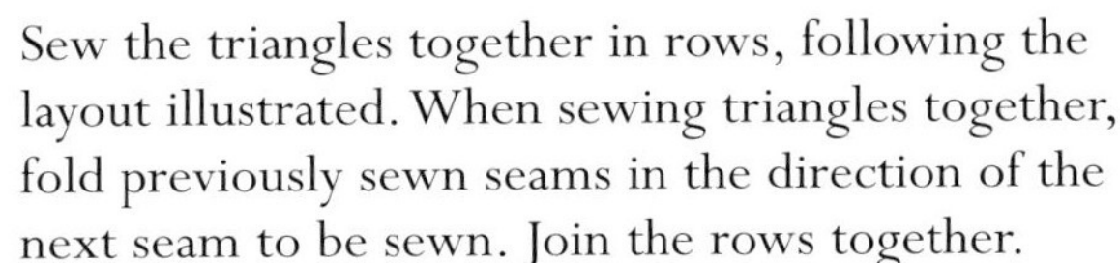

1 Sew the triangles together in rows, following the layout illustrated. When sewing triangles together, fold previously sewn seams in the direction of the next seam to be sewn. Join the rows together.

2 Follow steps 2 to 5 as for the Tea Cosy, except for step 3, when all sides of the triangles should be quilted.

PLACE MAT

If you wanted the lace to show up more on, you could use a pale blue fabric beneath the lace instead of the white.

Finished measurements:
43 x 33cm (17 x 13in)

MATERIALS

- 20cm (8in) blue and white chintz
- 50cm (20in) different blue and white (or the same) chintz
- 2.25m ($2\frac{1}{2}$yd) white cotton lace, 3cm ($1\frac{1}{4}$in) wide
- 10cm (4in) plain white cotton
- 50cm (20in) wadding/batting
- white thread

PREPARATION

Cut the following pieces:

- **Blue and white chintz**
  1 rectangle 12 x 22cm ($4\frac{3}{4}$ x $8\frac{3}{4}$in) for the centre
- **Second blue and white chintz**
  1 rectangle 40 x 50cm ($15\frac{3}{4}$ x $19\frac{3}{4}$in) for the backing
  strips 5cm (2in) wide, cut to required length as you sew
- **White fabric**
  strips 5cm (2in) wide, cut to required length as you sew
- **Wadding/batting.**
  1 rectangle 43 x 33cm (17 x 13in)

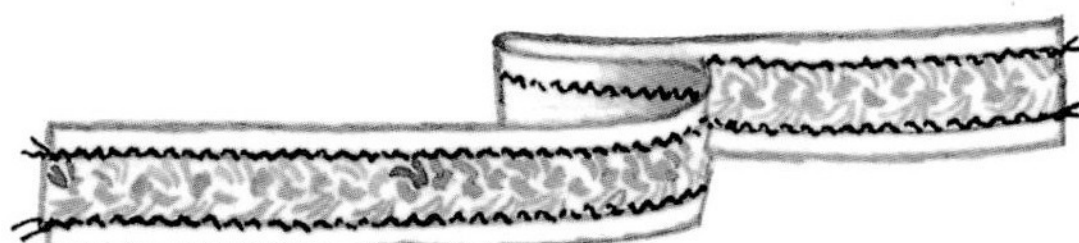

1 Centre the lace on the white strip and stitch in place with zigzag stitch or straight stitch.

2 Cut two lace strips to the same length as the centre rectangle and stitch in place. Measure the width of the rectangle and cut two lace strips to the same length. Stitch in place.

3 Repeat step 2 with a blue border strip, and then with a second lace border strip. Pin the completed patchwork to the wadding/batting and to the backing. Quilt along the seam lines, then trim the wadding/batting if necessary. Bind the mat, following the instructions in the Techniques section for self-binding with backing, and mitre the corners. Stitch into the corners as you stitch round the rectangle.

PROVENÇAL TABLECLOTH

This tablecloth, with its strong Mediterranean colours, is ideal for an outdoor lunch. It could equally well double up as a chair throw. It is very important to press the seams open after stitching each seam so that the cloth remains flat with as few ridges as possible.

Ciel Décor's Olives Niçoise fabric in green and yellow was used for this tablecloth. This has bands of different patterns which can be cut into strips. Ciel Décor is based in London, but a mail order service is available. If you are unable to obtain this material, improvise with other blue, yellow and green floral fabrics.

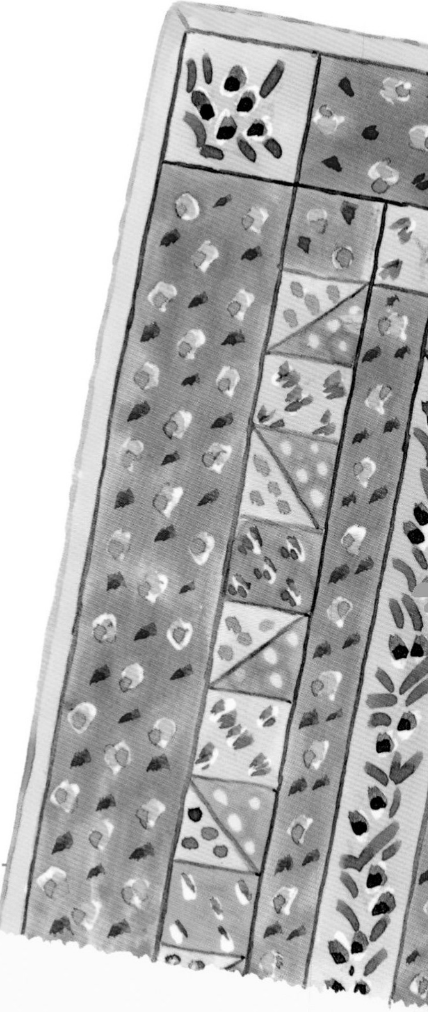

Finished measurements:
1.58 x 2m (62¼ x 78½in)

MATERIALS

- 1 9cm (3½in) square template and 1 right-angled triangle, with short sides 9.5cm (3¾in)
- 2m (2½yd) blue floral fabric
- 150cm (60in) fabric in a green colourway
- 150cm (60in) fabric in a yellow colourway
- 3.5m (4yd) cotton ticking
- 8m (9yd) yellow bias binding, 2cm (¾in) wide
- yellow thread

PREPARATION

Cut the following pieces:

- **Blue fabric**
  1 rectangle 18 x 58cm (7 x 22¾in)

  strips 6.5cm (2¾in) wide for borders

  4 strips, each 14.5cm (5¾in) wide by the length of the fabric, for outer border

  8 squares, cut using the template

- **Pink on green colourway**
  3 strips, each 9cm (3½in) wide, cut along the length of the fabric

  12 squares, cut using the template

- **Yellow on green colourway**
  72 triangles, cut using the template

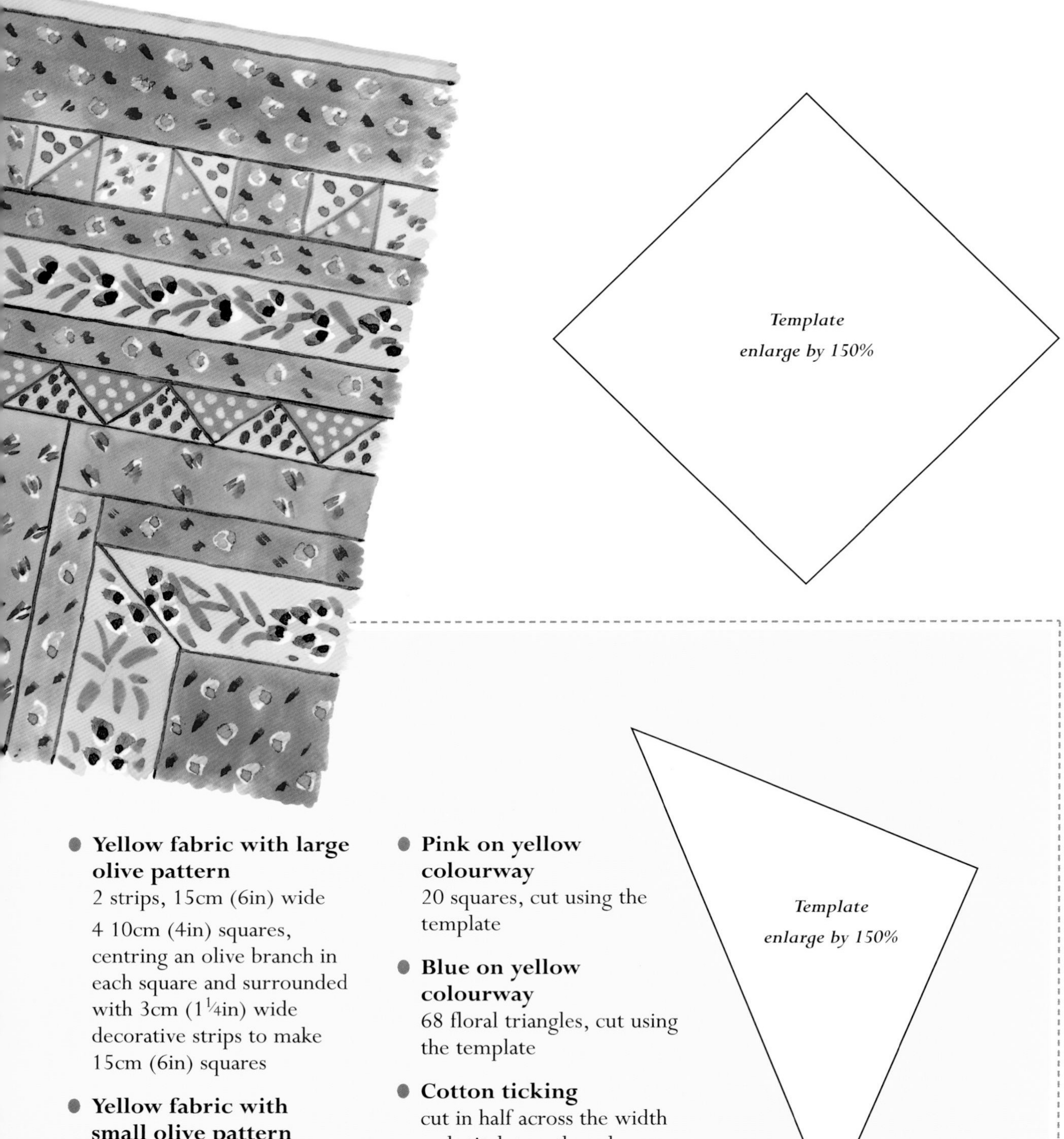

- **Yellow fabric with large olive pattern**
  2 strips, 15cm (6in) wide
  4 10cm (4in) squares, centring an olive branch in each square and surrounded with 3cm (1¼in) wide decorative strips to make 15cm (6in) squares

- **Yellow fabric with small olive pattern**
  4 strips, 9.5cm (3¾in) wide

- **Pink on yellow colourway**
  20 squares, cut using the template

- **Blue on yellow colourway**
  68 floral triangles, cut using the template

- **Cotton ticking**
  cut in half across the width and stitch together along the long sides

1 Lay the large olive border around the central blue rectangle, with the ends centred along the length of the rectangle. Make a 45-degree fold at the corners. Cut along the angle of the fold, remembering to allow for the 6mm (¼in) seam. Repeat with the other end, with the border ends overlapping each other by a seam allowance of 6mm (¼in).

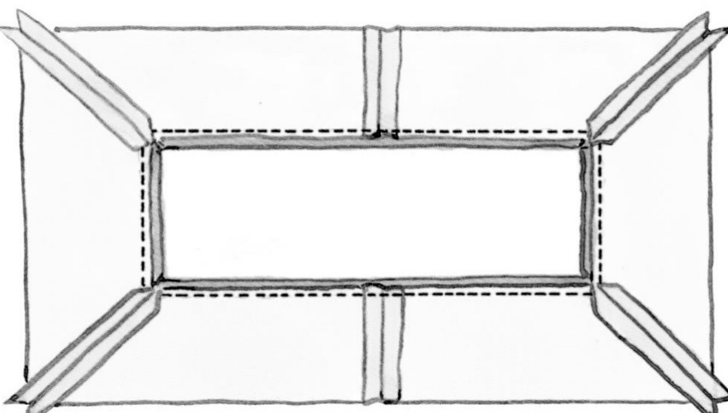

2 Join the two straight ends of the border together, then stitch along the long edges of the rectangle. Stitch the borders along the short edges. Sew the diagonals together, taking care not to pucker the inner rectangle. Add a blue border, then the pink on green strip, stitching the short edges before the long ones.

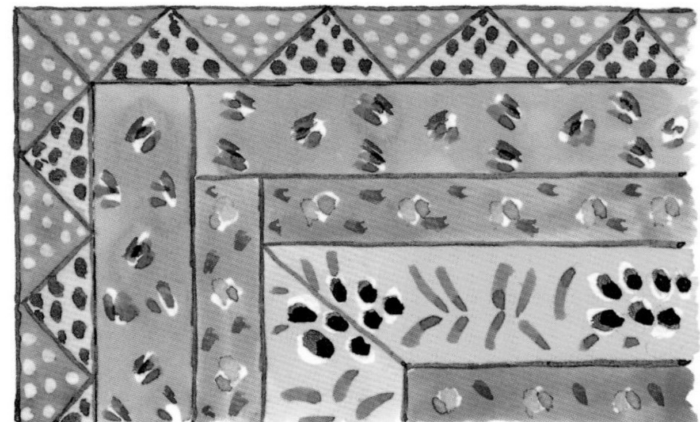

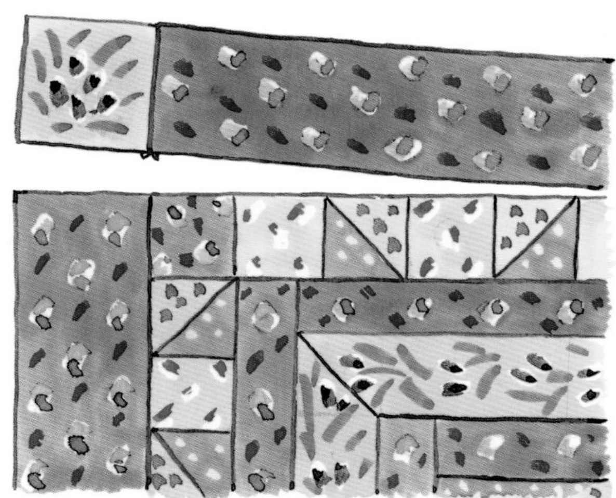

3 To make the triangle border, chain sew six yellow and green triangles along the short sides. Cut them apart, then stitch them together to form a row, adding a further green triangle at one end. Repeat. Attach to the two short edges of the patchwork along the base of the yellow triangles. For the long edges, stitch 10 yellow to 11 green triangles, repeat, then attach to the patchwork, joining green triangles together at the corners.

5 Measure the patchwork and cut two wide blue borders the same length as the short edge, and two the same as the long edges. Stitch the borders to both short edges. Stitch the yellow olive squares to the ends of the long strips, and then join them to the patchwork, matching the seams at the corners.

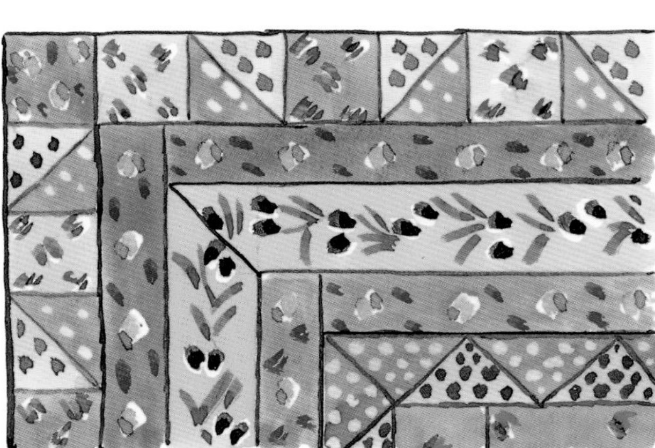

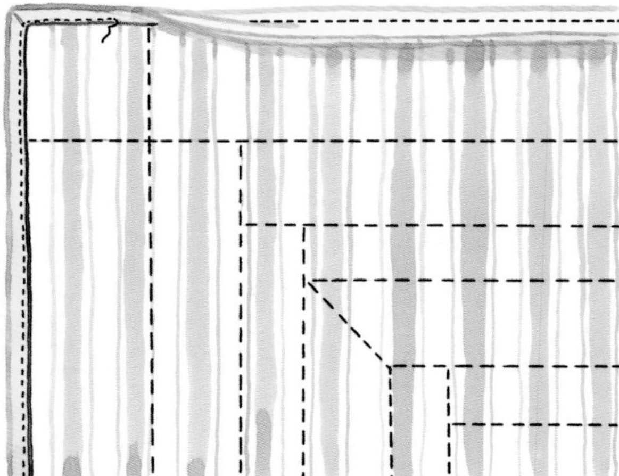

4 Add a blue border, then the narrow olive border (following the same procedure as the wide olive border). Add a further blue border. To make the patch border, chain sew green and yellow triangles together to form a square. Press and lay the square template on top of each pieced square. Draw round the template, and cut to even the edges. Piece together as illustrated.

6 Pin the patchwork to the cotton ticking and stitch along each border seam. Bind the edges with bias binding.

Log Cabin Cushion

The materials given are for a cushion to match the Log Cabin Throw (see pages 85–8). An alternative effect can be achieved by using light and dark fabrics and placing them opposite each other. The red square at the centre represents the hearth of the home and is a traditional feature of this pattern.

Finished measurements:
41 x 41cm (16 x 16in)

MATERIALS

- 12cm (5in) green floral fabric
- 12cm (5in) green check fabric
- 12cm (5in) russet floral fabric
- 12cm (5in) russet check fabric
- 12cm (5in) cream and russet floral fabric
- 12cm (5in) cream and russet check fabric
- 12cm (5in) green velvet
- 15cm (6in) dark russet fabric
- 41cm (16in) terracotta cotton
- 41cm (16in) square scrap fabric
- 180cm (70in) piping cord
- square cushion pad to fit finished patchwork
- green or russet thread

PREPARATION

Cut the following pieces:

- **Green floral fabric**
  4 strips, each 4 x 45cm (1½ x 18in)
- **Green check fabric**
  4 strips, each 4 x 45cm (1½ x 18in)
- **Russet floral fabric**
  4 strips, each 4 x 25cm (1½ x 10in)
- **Russet check fabric**
  4 strips, each 4 x 25cm (1½ x 10in)
- **Cream and russet floral fabric**
  4 strips, each 4 x 35cm (1½ x 14in)
- **Cream and russet check fabric**
  4 strips, each 4 x 35cm (1½ x 14in)
- **Green velvet**
  4 strips, each 5 x 45cm (2 x 18in)
- **Dark russet fabric**
  1 12cm (4¾in) square
  1 strip 4 x 180cm (1½ x 70in) for piping
- **Terracotta cotton**
  2 rectangles, each 41 x 32cm (16 x 12½in), for cushion back

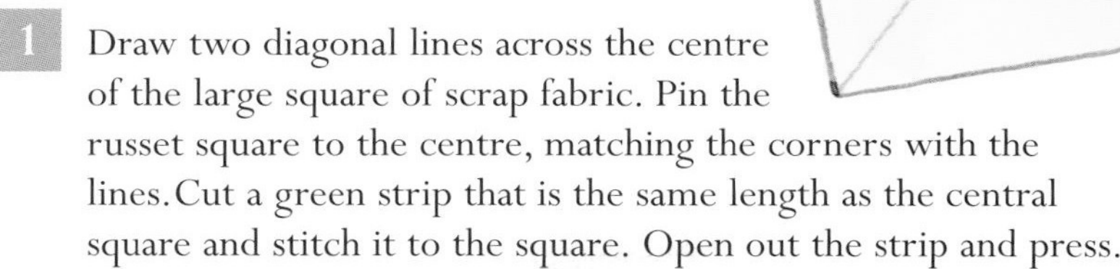

1 Draw two diagonal lines across the centre of the large square of scrap fabric. Pin the russet square to the centre, matching the corners with the lines. Cut a green strip that is the same length as the central square and stitch it to the square. Open out the strip and press.

2 Cut another green strip that is the same length as the central square plus the first strip, and stitch it in place.

3 Continue with two further green strips. Make sure that the corners of the square are aligned with the diagonal lines. Continue adding strips in the same order as for the Log Cabin Throw (see pages 85–8). When complete, trim so that the patchwork is 41cm (16in) square.

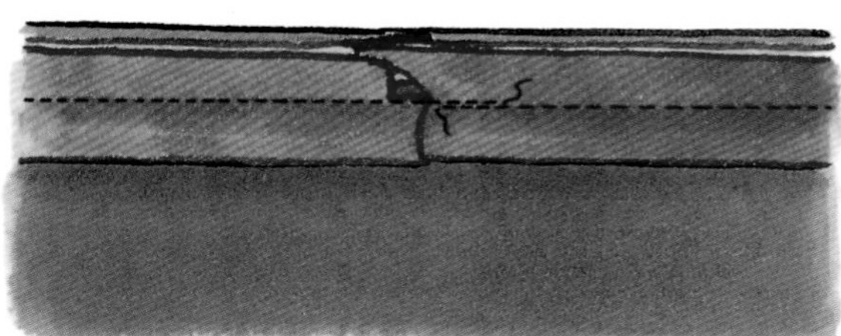

4 Wrap the dark russet strip around the piping cord and pin to the right side of the patchwork, matching raw edges. Machine stitch close to the piping, using a zipper foot, leaving 1cm (½in) at the beginning unstitched. Round the corners slightly. Cut the russet strip and cord to 2.5cm (1in) beyond the start of the piping. Fold under the raw edge of the end of the strip and wrap it around the start of the piping. Stitch to just beyond the start of the stitched line.

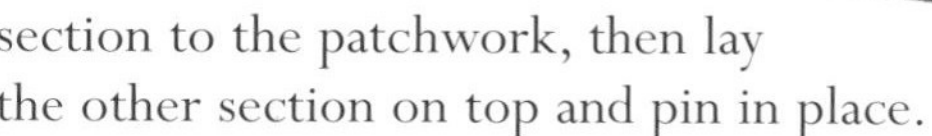

5 Fold under twice one raw edge of each cushion back section along the 41cm (16in) length and stitch. With right sides together, pin one cushion back section to the patchwork, then lay the other section on top and pin in place.

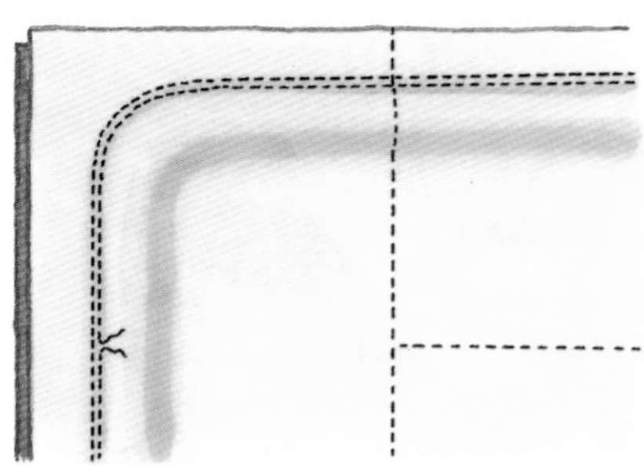

6 Stitch together, with the patchwork on top so that you can follow the stitching line of the piping. Turn right side out, then insert a square cushion pad through the opening at the back.

An alternative effect using light and dark fabrics.

Crazy Patchwork Cushion

Use any scraps of material that you have left over – you can even incorporate trimmings from other patchwork projects. Experiment with juxtaposing colours and patterns until you are happy with the arrangement. Dimensions have not been given, because these will depend on the cushion size you are using. If you do not have a zigzag option on your sewing machine, fold under the raw edges as you go and top-stitch in place.

MATERIALS

- scraps of fabric
- 1 square, 5cm (2cm) larger all round than your cushion pad, for the base
- 2 pieces of fabric the same width as the cushion and 20cm (8in) longer than half the length of the cushion, for the back
- 1 strip the length of the perimeter of the cushion plus 10cm (4in), 4cm (1½in) wide, for piping
- piping cord same length as piping strip
- cushion pad
- matching thread

1 Lay one of the scrap pieces at one corner of the base square. Pin in place. Lay the second patch slightly overlapping the first piece and zigzag along the raw edge.

2 Alternatively, fold under the raw edges and top-stitch in place.

3 Continue with the above process until you have covered the entire cushion base. Trim the patchwork and the base to the correct size for your cushion pad. Follow the piping and assembly instructions as for the Log Cabin Cushion steps 4 to 6 (see page 69).

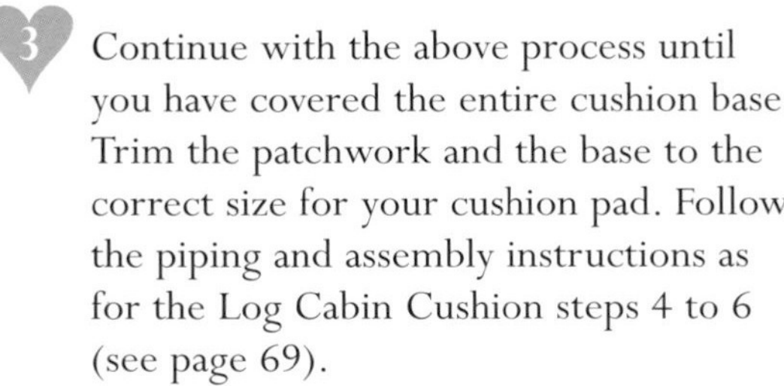

DOLL'S SHOOFLY QUILT

This little coverlet is tied rather than quilted. You could increase the number of blocks to 42 to make a cot quilt.

Finished measurements:
31 x 46cm (12 x 18in)

MATERIALS

- 2 templates, 6cm (2½in) and 5cm (2in) square
- 20cm (8in) red floral fabric
- 20cm (8in) white floral fabric
- 41cm (16in) plain white fabric
- 41cm (16in) wadding/batting
- skein neutral-coloured embroidery silk
- white thread

PREPARATION

Cut the following pieces:

- **Red floral fabric**
  12 6cm (2½in) squares
  6 5cm (2in) squares
  4 strips, each 4 x 13cm (1½ x 5in)
  3 strips, each 4 x 41cm (1½ x 16in)
  2 strips, each 4 x 30cm (1½ x 12in)
- **White floral fabric**
  12 6cm (2½in) squares
  24 5cm (2in) squares
  1 strip 4 x 160cm (1½ x 64in) for the binding
- **White fabric**
  1 rectangle 48 x 33cm (19 x 13in) for the backing
- **Wadding/batting**
  1 rectangle 48 x 33cm (19 x 13in)

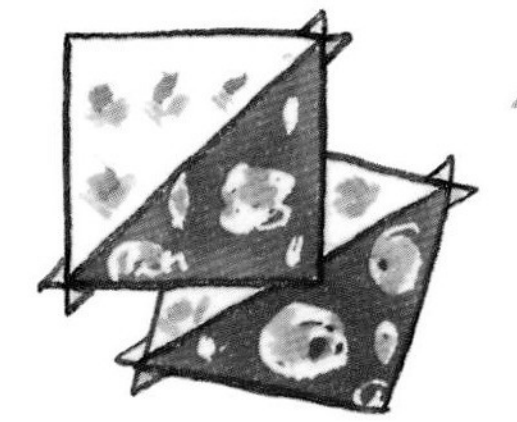

1 To make one Shoofly block, cut two red and two white 6cm (2½in) squares in half diagonally, and stitch the red triangles to the white triangles along the diagonal to form four squares.

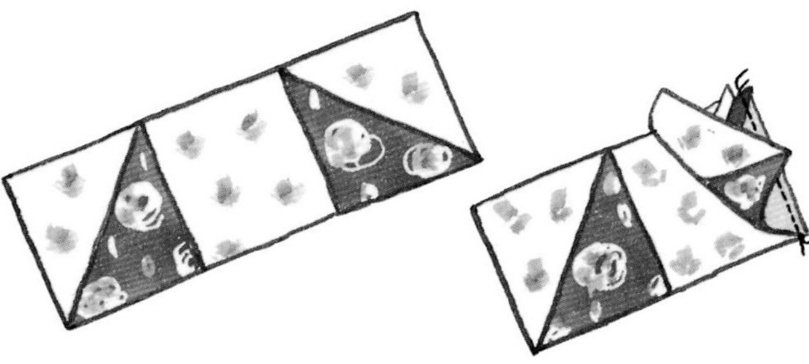

2 Stitch a pieced square on each side of a white 5cm (2in) square with the red triangles pointing in towards centre. Repeat with the other two pieced squares.

3 Stitch two white 5cm (2in) squares on each side of a red 5cm (2in) square.

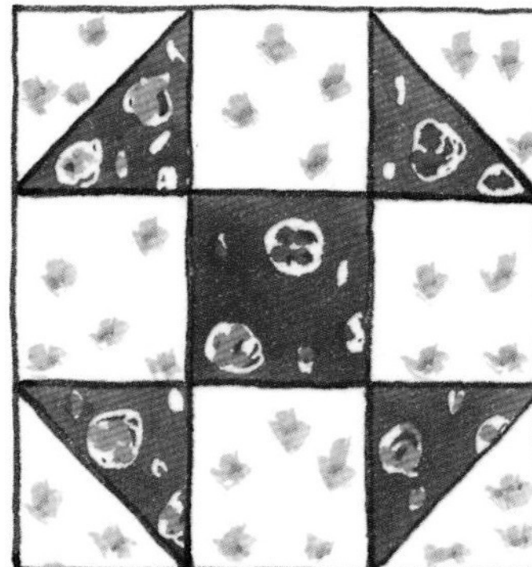

4 Join the rows together as illustrated, matching seams.

5 Repeat steps 1 to 4 five more times, so that you have six blocks in total. Join three blocks together with two short strips. Trim the strips. Repeat with the remaining three blocks.

6 Join the two rows together with the 41cm (16in) strip, making sure that the blocks are exactly aligned. Stitch two more strips to the long edges of the rows. Trim the strips. Stitch the two 31cm (12in) strips to the top and bottom of the patchwork.

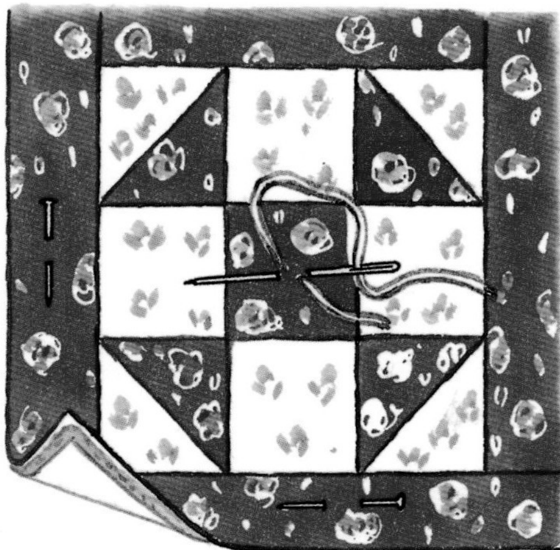

7 Lay the backing fabric, wrong side up, on a large, flat surface, placing the wadding/batting on top, with the patchwork, right side up, on top of that. Pin the layers together. Thread an unknotted strand of silk on a needle and make two backstitches through all three layers at the centre of a red square, leaving a tail 2cm (¾in) long.

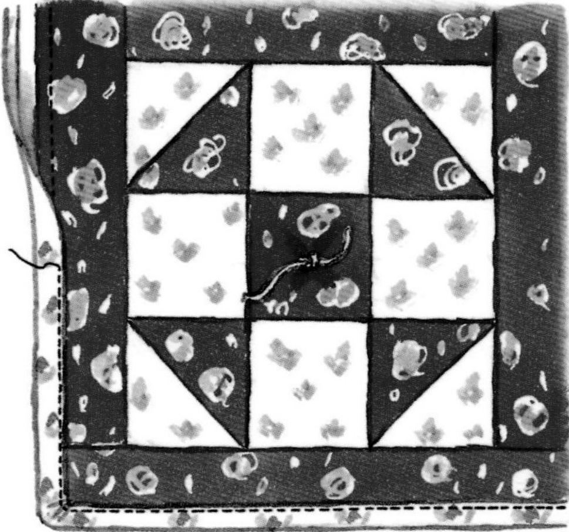

8 Pull the thread tight and tie a double knot. Cut the thread ends to 1cm (½in). Repeat on all red and pieced squares and down the central strip at even intervals. Trim the backing and wadding. Bind the quilt following the strip binding instructions in the Techniques section, easing the binding around the corners.

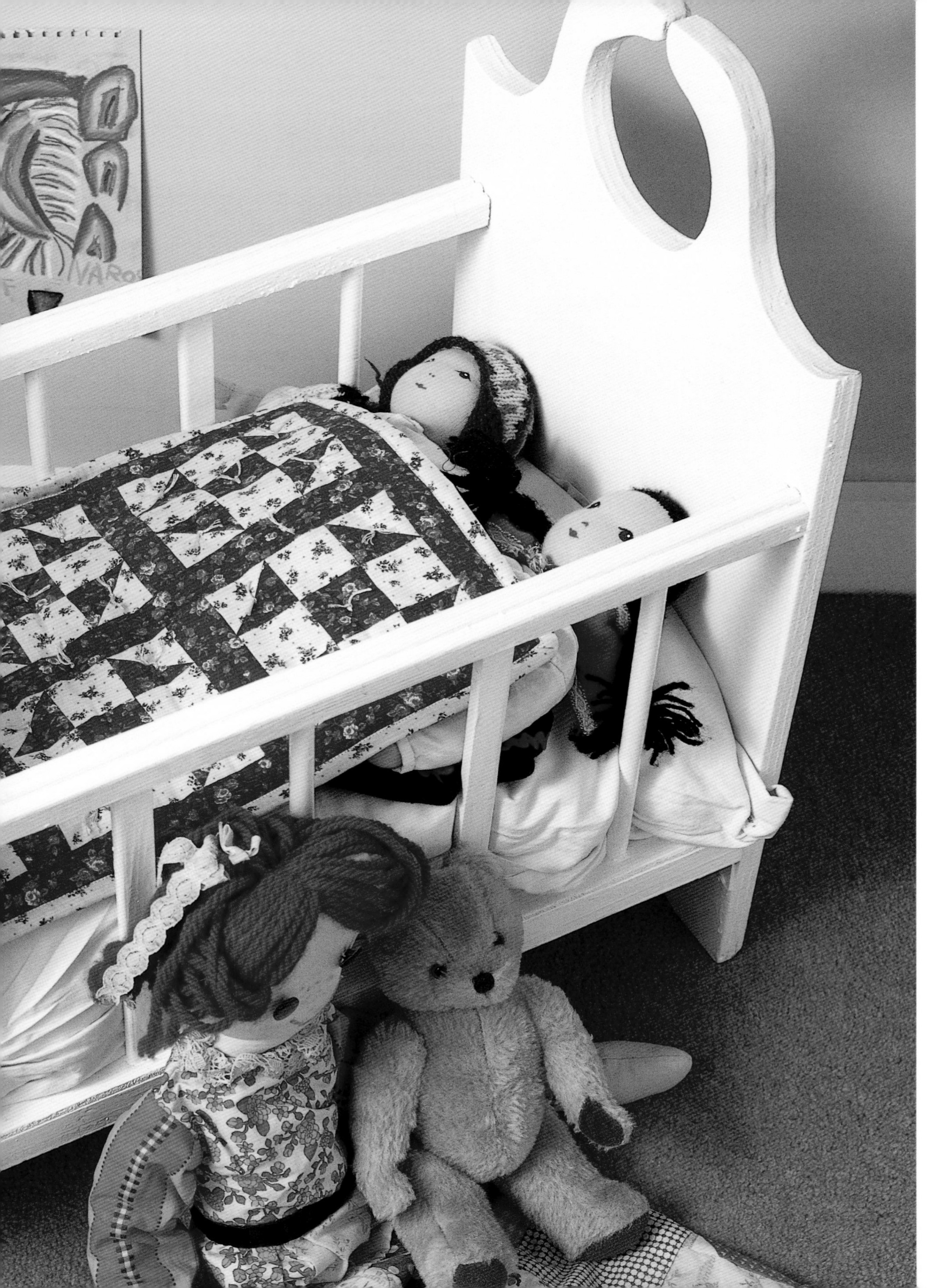

Picnic Rug

This picnic rug, which could also be used as a mat for a play pen, is very quick and easy to make. Because the fabric is handwoven, the checks may not align, but do not worry about this – it is these irregularities that add to the rug's charm and simplicity.

Finished measurements: 1.42 x 1.42m (56 x 56in), excluding fringe

MATERIALS

- 1m (1yd) Laura Ashley Mitford Check, deep pink
- 2m (2yd) Laura Ashley Mitford Check, chambray
- 1.5m (60in) blue PVC fabric, 144cm (57in) wide
- 3m (3yd) wadding/batting
- 3m (3yd) muslin or thin cotton
- yellow and blue threads

PREPARATION

Cut the following pieces:

- **Pink check fabric**
  8 36cm (14¼in) squares
- **Chambray check fabric**
  8 36cm (14¼in) squares (cut the squares at least 2 checks in from the selvedges)

  2 border strips, each 8cm x 1.5m (3⅛ x 60in) along the selvedges (i.e., 1 check in from selvedge)

  2 border strips, each 6cm x 1.5m (2¼ x 60in) (i.e., 1 check wide)
- **Wadding/batting**
  cut in half and stitch the 2 pieces together along the length; trim to 1.5 x 1.5m (60 x 60in)
- **Muslin**
  cut in half and stitch the 2 pieces together along the length, trim to 1.5 x 1.5m (60 x 60in)

1 Stitch four rows of four squares together, alternating blue and pink fabrics. Join the rows together.

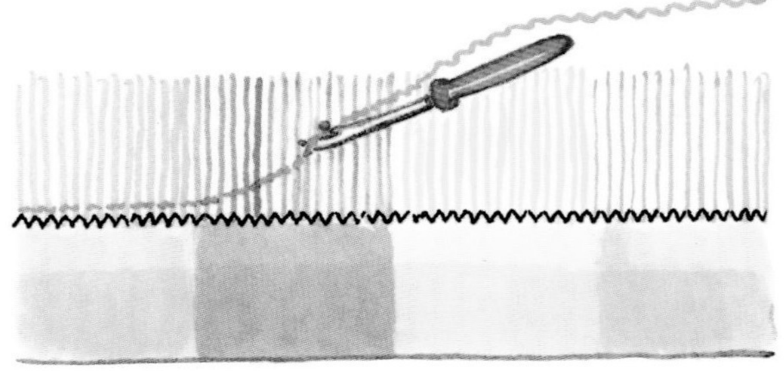

2 Set the machine to small zigzag (or small straight stitch if you do not have this option) and stitch along the centre of the 8cm (3⅛in) border strips. Use a stitch unpicker to pull out the warp threads from the selvedge to the stitching line to leave a fringe of coloured threads.

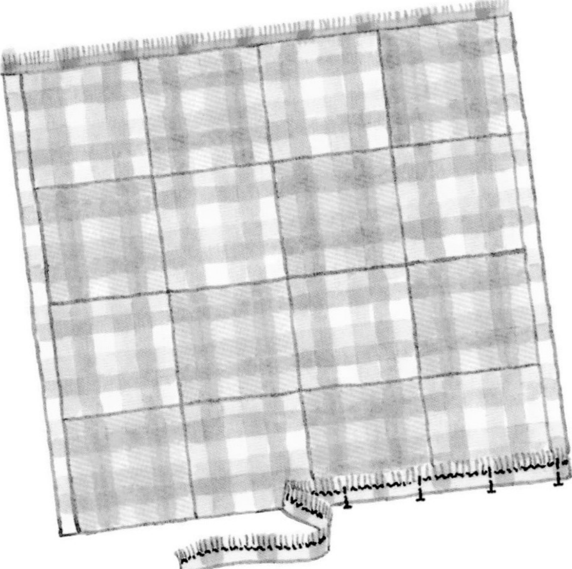

3 Stitch the 6cm (2¼in) borders to opposite sides of the patchwork. Trim. Sew the fringe strips to the patchwork.

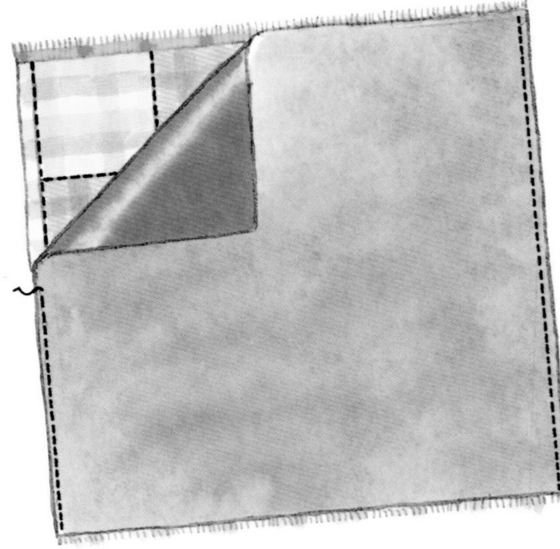

4 Sandwich the wadding/batting between the muslin and the patchwork and pin the layers together. Quilt along all the seam lines. Lay the PVC on top of the patchwork, with right sides together. Trim. Pin together, then stitch along the two unfringed edges of the patchwork. Turn right side out.

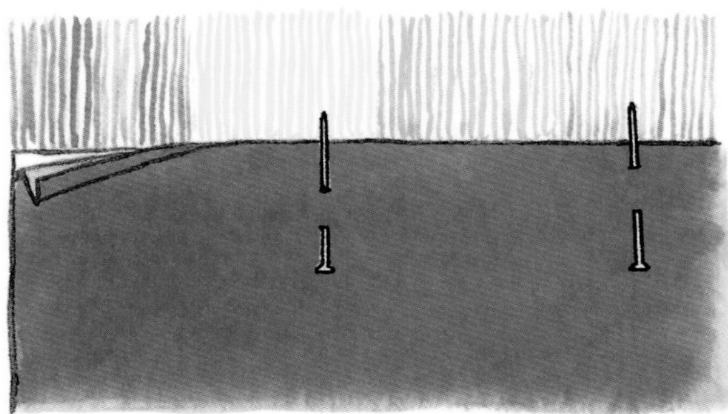

5 Turn under the PVC beneath the fringe to enclose the wadding, keeping the fold in line with the start of the fringe. Pin in position. With yellow thread on the machine and blue thread on the bobbin, top-stitch the patchwork to the PVC, keeping your stitching line close to the fringe.

DRAWING ROOM THROW

This throw is elegant yet simple to make, and although the fabrics used are expensive, they are nonetheless cheaper than having a sofa recovered. If you use the fabrics listed below, the throw will have to be dry cleaned.

Finished measurements:
1.9 x 2.82m (75 x 111in)

MATERIALS

- 2 square window templates 20.5cm (8in) and 12cm (4¾in)
- 4m (4½yd) Laura Ashley Bryony (russet), linen union
- 3m (3¼yd) Laura Ashley Mallory Stripe (brick), woven stripe
- 4m (4½yd) calico, 186cm (73½in) wide
- white or cream thread

PREPARATION

Cut the following pieces:

- **Bryony fabric.**
  54 roses; using the large window template, centre roses with stems pointing down, draw round the template and cut out

  40 rosebuds; using the small window template, centre as above.

Note: It is not always possible to cut the roses on the straight grain and a certain amount of manoeuvring of the templates will be required. Every large rose, apart from those next to the selvedges, can be used with this size template. Although it is necessary to cut into some rosebuds, because fewer of these are required there are enough left over.

- **Mallory Stripe fabric**
  87 sashes, each 12 x 20.5cm (4¾ x 8in) (cut down the centre of each of the middle white stripes so that the pale band is centred on the sash)

  2 sashes, each 12 x 260cm (4¾ x 102½in), for the long borders

  2 sashes 12 x 195cm (4¾ x 77in), for the short borders.

- **Calico**
  cut in half across the width and stitch along the two lengths

Template
enlarge by 400%

Template
enlarge by 400%

1 Stitch together nine roses (alternating colours) separated by eight vertical sashes. Because these fabrics fray, stitch the raw edges of the seams together with a zigzag or a close straight stitch throughout.

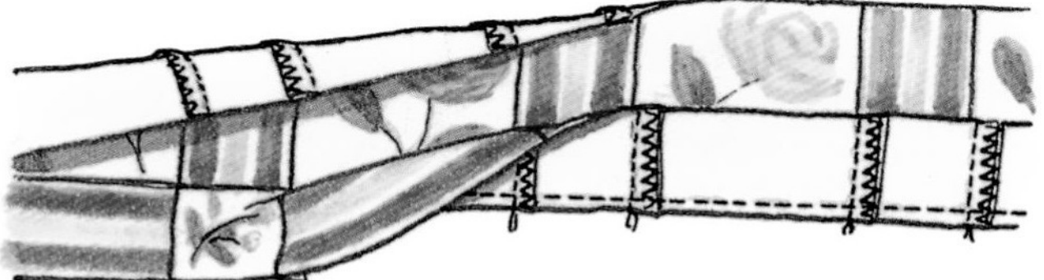

2 Stitch together nine horizontal sashes separated by eight rosebuds. Pin the row of roses to the row of rosebuds, matching the seams (lay the seams in opposite directions to avoid bulk). Stitch.

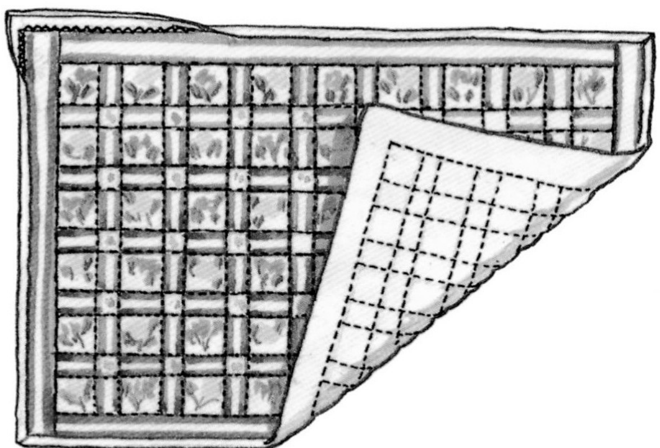

3 Repeat steps 1 and 2 until you have six rows of roses separated by five rows of rosebuds. Stitch the two long border sashes along both long edges and the two shorter border sashes along the short edges. Trim and finish the raw edges of the borders as above. With wrong sides together, pin the patchwork to the calico and quilt along the seam lines, using a long machine stitch. Trim the calico so that it overlaps by 4cm (1½in) all the way round. Bind, following the instructions in the Techniques section for self-binding with backing. Mitre the corners.

Ohio Star Single Quilt

Old tartan shirts, pyjamas and trousers were used to make the stars for this quilt, which is based on the traditional American pattern. Each star block is made from eight triangles and one central square cut from the same fabric plus eight white triangles and four white squares.

Finished measurements: 2.15 x 2.55m (84½ x 100in)

MATERIALS

- 3 templates, 12cm (4¾in), 15.5cm (6in) and 43cm (17in) square
- various tartan-patterned old clothes; if you are buying the fabrics, 30cm (12in) is enough for three star blocks (there are 15 in all)
- 2.5m (3yd) calico
- 3.5m (4yd) dark blue floral fabric
- 6m (6½yd) green and blue tartan fabric for backing
- 5m (5½yd) wadding/batting
- blue thread

PREPARATION

Cut the following pieces:

- **Calico**
  60 12cm (4¾in) squares; press each square in half diagonally and cut along the fold to give 120 triangles

  60 15.5cm (6in) squares
- **Tartan fabric**
  60 12cm (4¾in) squares; press each square in half diagonally and cut along the fold to give 120 triangles

  15 15.5cm (6in) squares
- **Dark blue floral fabric**
  15 43cm (17in) squares
- **Backing fabric**
  cut in half across width and stitch together along length
- **Wadding/batting**
  cut in half across the width and stitch together along length

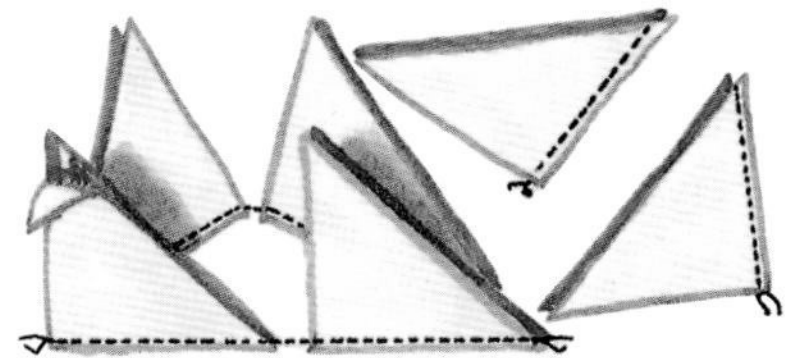

To make a star block, sew a calico triangle to a tartan triangle along one short edge. Making sure the calico triangle is always uppermost, chain sew seven further pairs of triangles. Cut apart. Clip the corners.

Join two pieced triangles together along the long edge to make a square. Repeat with the remaining triangles, making a total of four pieced squares.

Sew a calico square on each side of a pieced square, attaching them along the tartan edges. Repeat. Sew the two remaining pieced squares, this time along the calico edge, on each side of a matching tartan central square. Join the three rows together.

Repeat steps 1 to 3 to make 14 further star blocks, using the same colour fabric for the triangles and central square each time. Make up three rows of three star blocks separated by two dark blue squares, then three rows of three dark blue squares separated by two star blocks. Alternate the rows and stitch them together, matching the seams.

Pin the patchwork to the wadding/batting and backing fabric. Quilt along the block seams. Trim the wadding. Trim the backing so that it overlaps by 13cm (5in) all the way round. Bind the quilt with the backing, following the instructions in the Techniques section for self-binding. Mitre the corners.

LOG CABIN THROW

The throw does not have wadding/batting, and it is, therefore, lighter than a bedspread. If you wanted to give it a more luxurious feel, you could use velvet fabrics for the plain sections.

Finished measurements:
2.6 x 1.7m (102 x 67in)

MATERIALS

- 1 template 12cm (4¾in) square
- 50cm (20in) each of 4 green cotton floral/check fabrics
- 25cm (10in) each of 4 russet cotton floral/check fabrics
- 25cm (10in) each of 4 cream and russet floral/check fabrics
- 1.5m (60in) bottle green needlecord or velvet
- 1m (1yd) plain dark russet cotton fabric
- 1.5m (60in) checked terracotta and green cotton fabric
- 7.5 (8yd) plain terracotta cotton fabric for backing and sashes
- matching thread

PREPARATION

It is easier to cut or rip the strips to the required length after they are sewn, rather than measuring and cutting them before stitching. For the longer sashes you will need to stitch widths together or cut sashes from the length of the backing fabric.

- **Green cotton fabrics**
  strips 4cm (1½in) wide cut across the width of the fabric
- **Russet cotton fabrics**
  strips 4cm (1½in) wide cut across the width of the fabric
- **Cream and russet fabrics**
  strips 4cm (1½in) wide cut across the width of the fabric
- **Needlecord or velvet**
  strips 4cm (1½in) wide cut along the length of the fabric
- **Dark russet fabric**
  15 12cm (4¾in) squares

  2 sashes, each 8 x 250cm (3 x 99in)

  2 sashes, each 8 x 180cm (3 x 71in)
- **Checked terracotta and green fabric**
  2 sashes, each 8 x 150cm (3 x 59in)

  2 sashes, each 8 x 250cm (3 x 99in)
- **Plain terracotta fabric**
  10 sashes, each 8 x 40cm (3 x 15¾in), cut across the width

  6 sashes, each 8 x 135cm (3 x 53in)

  2 sashes, each 8 x 235cm (3 x 92½in)

  cut remaining fabric in half across the width and stitch together to make a rectangle 1.9 x 2.8m (75 x 110in)

1 Stitch one green patterned strip to a russet square. Cut the strip so it is even with the square.

2 Turn the square so the first strip is along the top edge of the square, then attach a second green patterned strip along the right edge. Trim the strip. Repeat with two more green strips.

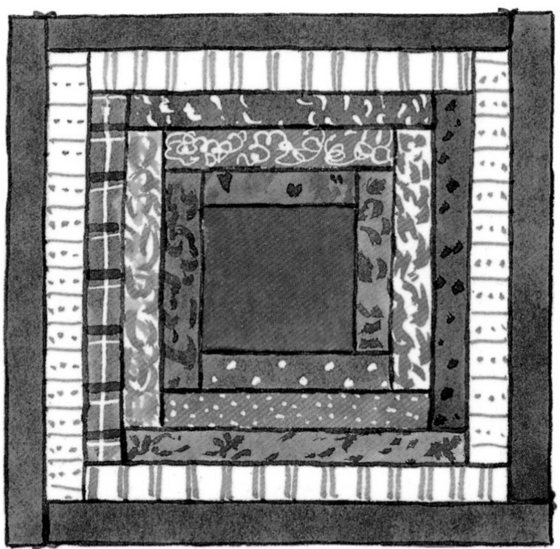

3 Stitch russet patterned strips around the pieced central square, then green patterned strips, then cream and russet strips and, finally, a green corduroy border.

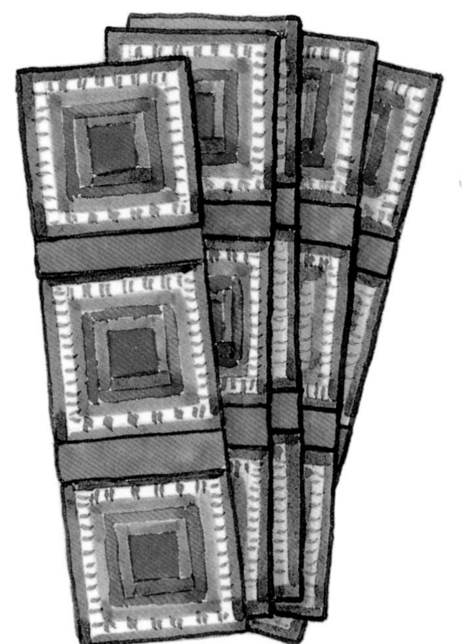

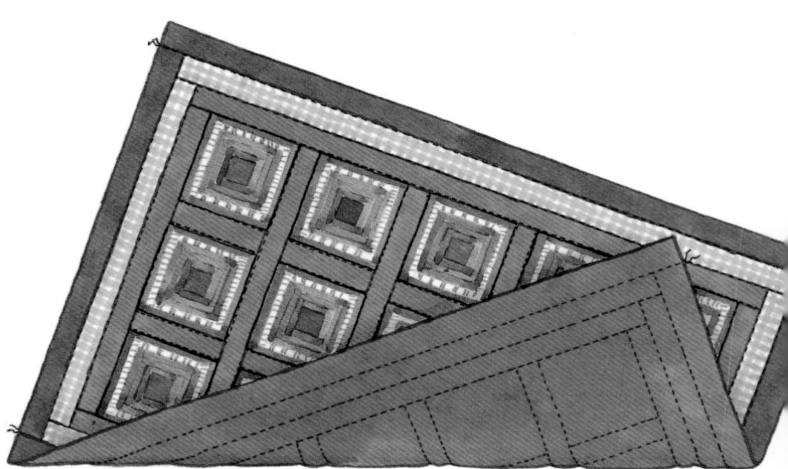

4 Repeat steps 1 to 3 to make 15 blocks in all. Join three blocks together by sewing two 40cm (15¾in) terracotta sashes between them. Repeat until you have five rows of three blocks.

6 Stitch the two long terracotta sashes along the two long sides of the patchwork. Sew the two shorter checked sashes along the short edges and the two longer checked sashes along the long edges. Repeat with the dark russet sashes. Press thoroughly. Lay the backing, wrong side up, on the floor. Lay the patchwork right side up on top. Pin, working from centre outwards, then quilt along all the seams.

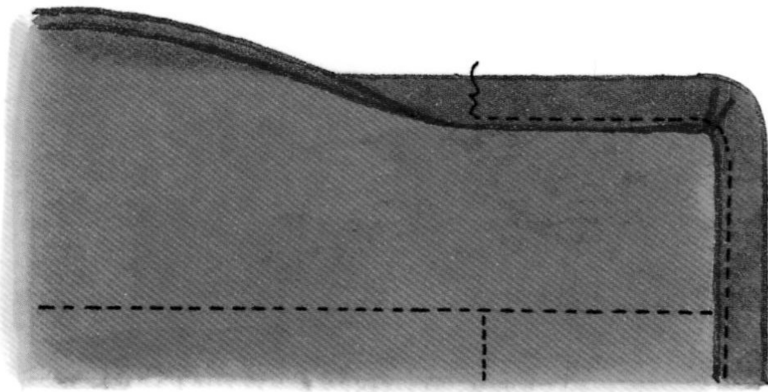

7 Trim the backing so that it is even with the quilt top. Bind with the quilt top using method outlined in the Techniques section for self-binding.

5 Join the five rows together with the 135cm (53in) terracotta sashes, attaching a sash at each end as well.

NINE-PATCH SINGLE QUILT

This single quilt is composed of 15 nine-patch blocks. The traditional red, white and blue colour scheme makes a bright cover for a child's bed, and if you wished, you could use navy sashes for a boy's bed and floral sashes for a girl's bed. You can vary the arrangement of the plain and patterned squares, and some suggestions are included in the list of materials.

MATERIALS

- 1 template 12cm ($4\frac{3}{4}$in) square
- 1m (1yd) navy floral fabric (or you can use different navy fabrics for each nine-patch block, as a guide, 15cm/6in is enough for two blocks)
- 1m (1yd) plain white fabric (you can also use a sparsely sprigged fabric on a white ground for the centre of eight of the blocks, for which you will need 15cm/6in)
- 30cm (12in) red and white gingham
- 41cm (16in) white on red spotted fabric
- 1.6m (2yd) navy fabric with a geometric or floral motif
- 4.5m (5yd) calico (or an old single sheet) for backing
- 4.5m (5yd) wadding/batting
- 1m (1yd) plain red brushed cotton for binding
- white and red threads

Finished measurements:
2.2 x 1.4m
($86\frac{1}{2}$ x 55in)

PREPARATION

Cut the following pieces:

- **Navy fabric**
  60 12cm ($4\frac{3}{4}$in) squares
- **White fabric**
  60 12cm ($4\frac{3}{4}$in) squares
- **Red and white gingham**
  15 12cm ($4\frac{3}{4}$in) squares
- **Red and white spotted fabric**
  24 12cm ($4\frac{3}{4}$in) squares
- **Navy geometric or floral fabric**
  38 sashes, each 12 x 33cm ($4\frac{3}{4}$ x 13in)
- **Backing fabric**
  cut in half across the width and stitch together along length
- **Binding fabric**
  cut or rip into 10cm (4in) strips; you will need 2 strips 2.2m (86in) long and 2 strips 1.5m (60in) long
- **Wadding/batting**
  cut in half across the width and stitch together along the length

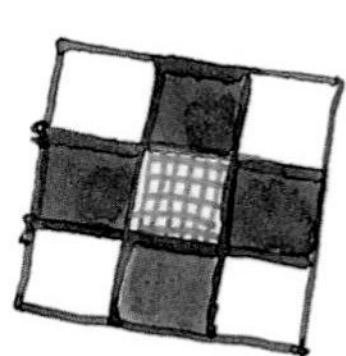

1 To make a block, stitch two white squares on each side of a navy square. Repeat. Stitch two navy squares on each side of a gingham one. Join the three rows together, matching seams. Repeat until you have 15 nine-patch blocks.

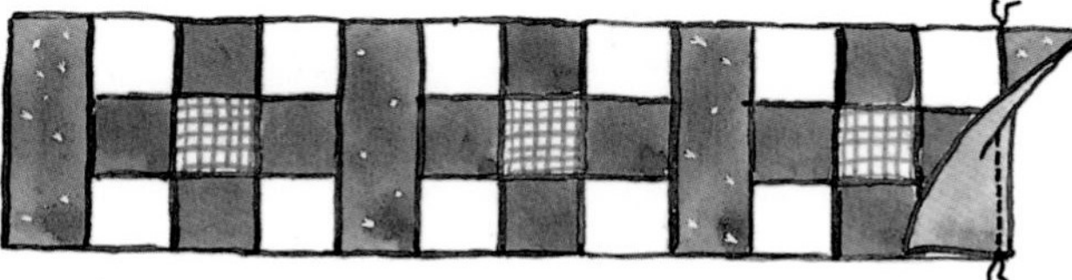

2 Make up a row of three blocks by stitching sashes between the blocks and at each end. Repeat four times, so that you have five rows in total.

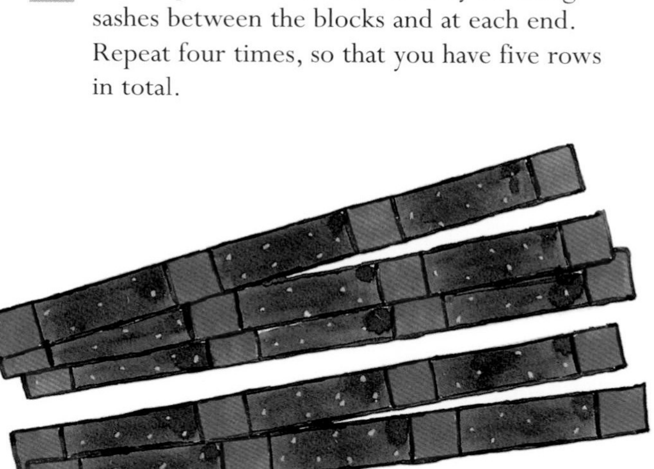

3 Alternate four red and white spotted squares with three sashes. Repeat five times, so that you have six strips in total.

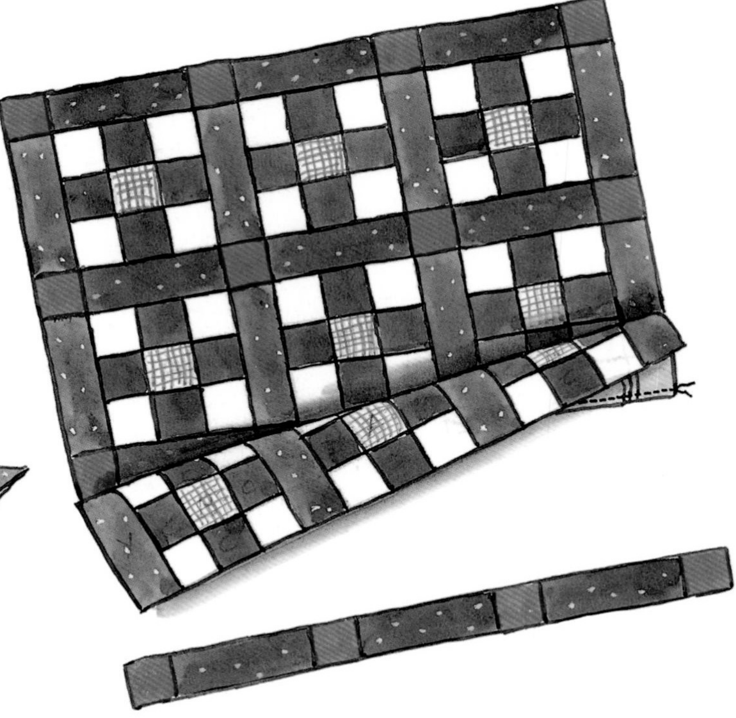

4 Join these to the long edges of the pieced-block rows, matching seams. Repeat until all the rows have been joined together.

5 Lay the patchwork on top of the wadding/batting and the backing. Press, pin and then baste together. Trim the wadding/batting and backing. Quilt diagonally or along the seam lines. Trim edges and bind as described in the Techniques section for binding with a strip.

Finished measurements:
2.85 x 1.55m (112 x 60in)

KILIM WALL HANGING

This wall hanging was inspired by the Oriental flat-weave rugs known as kilims. Material quantities have not been given, because the way you build up your quilt will depend on the pattern of the fabric you use and the size of the motifs. Use the instructions as a guide and experiment with different arrangements.

MATERIALS

- 'ethnic' patterned fabrics, most probably obtained from a furnishing fabric shop or department; choose a fabric that has a large motif, which can be cut out and bordered by plain fabrics
- strips of smaller patterned fabrics that can be used as borders; these could be made up from a discontinued fabric sample book because it does not matter if the colourways differ
- wider strips in ethnic fabrics for inner and outer borders
- plain fabrics in three or more complimentary colours (we used reddish-brown, blue and beige)
- blanket for backing
- binding strip, 5cm (2in) wide, cut to the same length as the perimeter of your quilt plus 10cm (4in)
- thick wool or garden twine for making fringes or use a ready-made fringe (optional)
- matching thread

PREPARATION

Cut the following pieces:

- **Main fabric**
  21 rectangular motifs
- **Plain fabrics**
  strips 6cm (2½in) wide for motif borders
- **Various ethnic patterns**
  strips 6cm (2½in) wide for borders

  strips 14cm (5½in) wide for inner and outer borders (use a different design)

1 Stitch plain border strips to the two short edges of a rectangular motif block. Trim the strips so that they are even with the block. Stitch two further strips along the long edges. Trim. Repeat until you have four blue-, nine reddish-brown- and eight beige-bordered blocks.

2 Stitch five blocks together along the long edges, separated by four narrow ethnic strips. Attach ethnic strips around the joined blocks to form a border around a panel composed of five blocks.

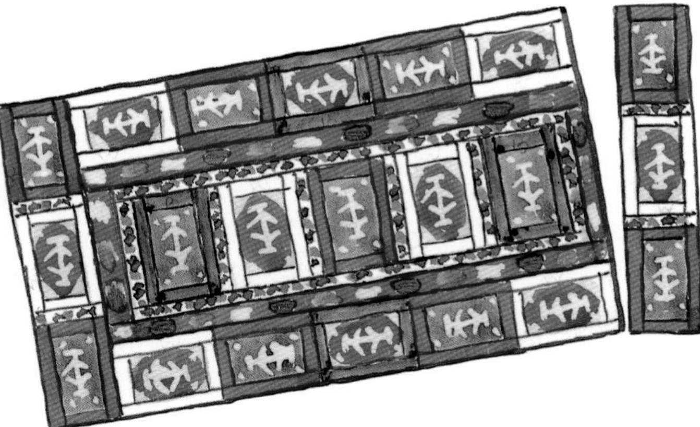

Stitch the wide strips around the central panel. Sew five blocks together along the short edges, then join these to the length of the central panel. Repeat with five more blocks and sew these to the other length. (You may need to add strips between the blocks or use fewer blocks so that they are the same length as the central panel). Join three blocks together along their short edges, separated by two 6cm ($2\frac{1}{2}$in) ethnic strips. Join these to one short edge of the central panel. Repeat and attach to the other short edge.

Stitch the wide border strip around the panel, then two narrower strips along both short edges. Pin and quilt to the blanket. Bind the edges with the binding strip, following the instructions in Techniques section. Knot garden twine or sew a ready-made fringe along the short edges, if desired.

ALTERNATIVE DESIGN

An alternative method of making a wall hanging is to create bands of different patterns and to join them together with strips of plain fabric.

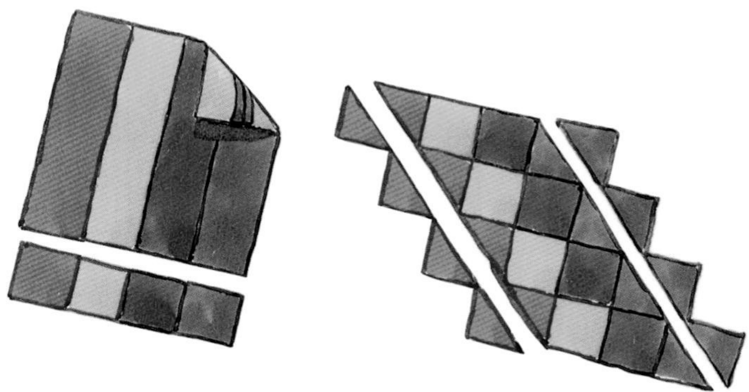

Stitch four long strips of different coloured fabrics together. Cut across the strips horizontally and rearrange them as illustrated. Trim the edges to make a strip of diamonds, which can also be used as a border.

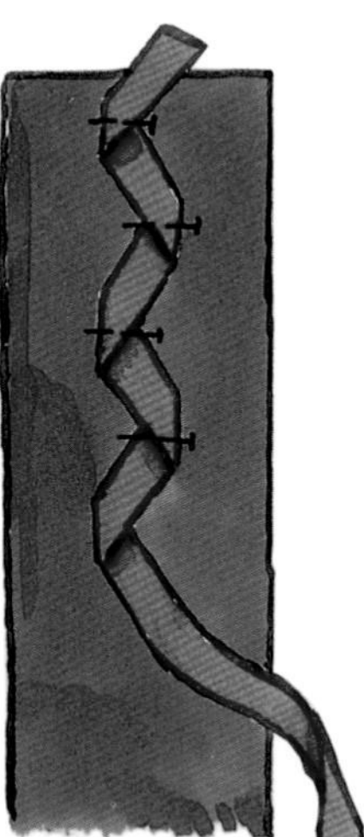

Fold a length of decorative braid into a zigzag pattern, arranging it along the centre of a strip of a plain fabric. Top-stitch in position.

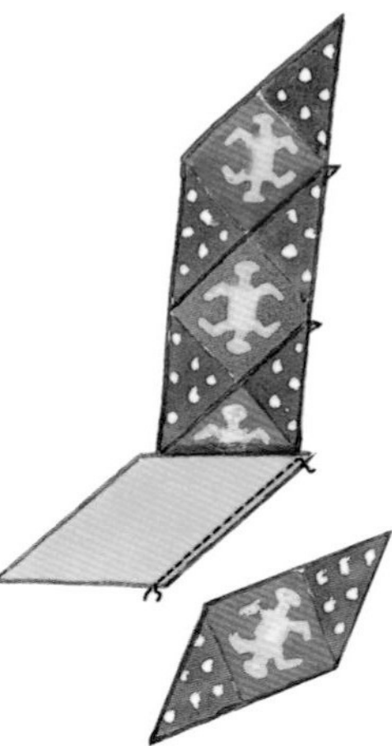

3 Cut out appropriately sized motifs from your chosen fabrics, stitch them together and attach plain borders.

4 Join the patterned bands with strips of plain fabric, trimmed to length, and finish off the wall hanging by adding a border of the diamond-patterned strip (see step 1).

EVENING STAR DOUBLE QUILT

If you are making this quilt for a bed with a footboard, make it four stars long, as shown on page 98. If you are making it for a single bed, make it four stars wide. You may prefer to buy the Laura Ashley ready-cut patchwork squares for this quilt; the squares needed are listed below.

MATERIALS

- 3 templates, 15.5cm (6¼in), 12cm (4¾in) and 11cm (4½in) square
- 1.2m (4ft) white on pink geometric fabric
- 3m (3yd) sparsely sprigged pink on white floral fabric
- 2.2m (2½yd) pink on white ticking
- 2.2m (2½yd) pink on white floral fabric
- 3.5m (4yd) plain pink fabric
- 60cm (24in) white on pink floral fabric
- 40cm (15in) plain white fabric
- 2m (2yd) candy stripe fabric
- 7.5m (8yd) floral or plain fabric for backing, cut and stitched together to make a square 2.5 x 2.5m (98 x 98in)
- 7.5m (8yd) wadding/batting
- white or pink thread

Finished measurements:
2.5 x 2.7m (98 x 116in)

PREPARATION

Cut the following pieces:

- **White on pink geometric fabric**
  80 12cm (4¾in) squares; press each square in half diagonally and cut along the fold to give 160 triangles
- **Sparsely sprigged pink on white floral fabric**
  70 12cm (4¾in) squares; press each square in half diagonally and cut along the fold to give 140 triangles
  80 11cm (4½in) squares
- **Pink on white ticking**
  60 12cm (4¾in) squares; press each square in half diagonally and cut along the fold to give 120 triangles
  80 11cm (4½in) squares
- **Pink on white floral fabric**
  60 11cm (4½in) squares
- **Plain pink fabric**
  40 12cm (4¾in) squares; press each square in half diagonally and cut along the fold to give 80 triangles
  15 15.5cm (6¼in) square
  120 11cm (4½in) squares

To make a pink-centred star, stitch eight pink geometric triangles to eight ticking triangles to form eight pieced squares. Stitch together two pieced squares, with the ticking triangles together, to form a rectangle with a large ticking triangle in the centre. Repeat with other pieced squares to make three further rectangles.

2 strips, each 6 x 150cm (2½ x 60cm), for borders

4 strips, each 5 x 250cm (2 x 60cm), for binding

- **White on pink floral fabric**
  40 11cm (4½in) squares
- **Plain white fabric**
  10 15.5cm (6¼in) squares
- **Candy striped fabric**
  120 11cm (4½in) squares

  2 strips, each 6 x 250cm (2½ x 98½in), for borders

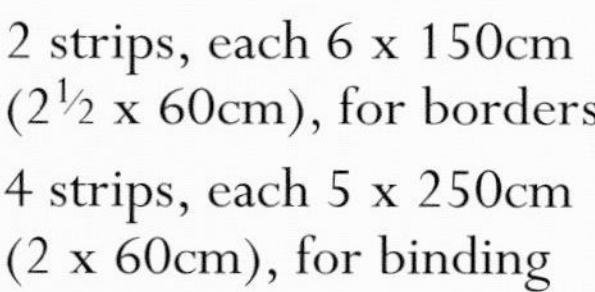

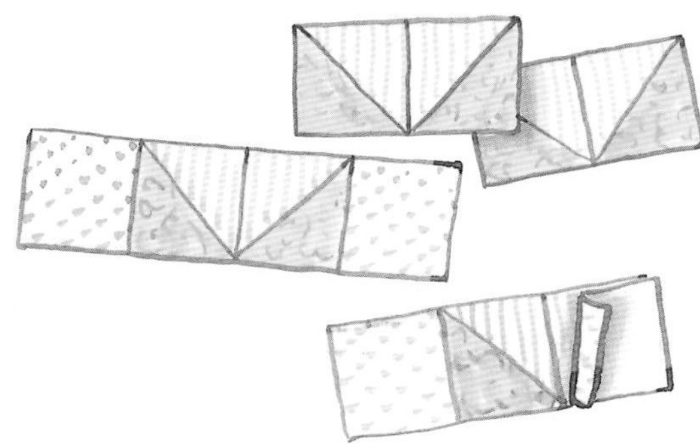

Stitch a pink on white floral square at each end of two of the pieced rectangles.

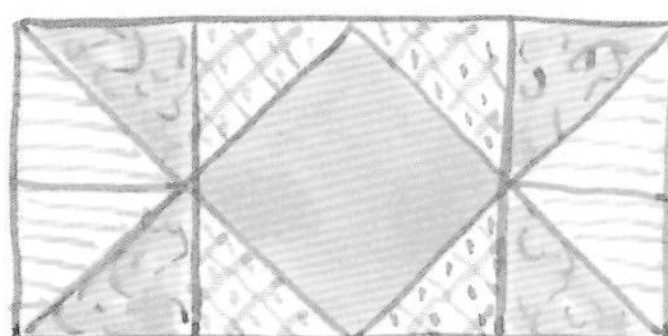

Stitch four sparsely sprigged triangles to each side of a plain pink square. Stitch the remaining two rectangles on either side of the pieced central square, with the points of the triangles meeting the points of the pink square.

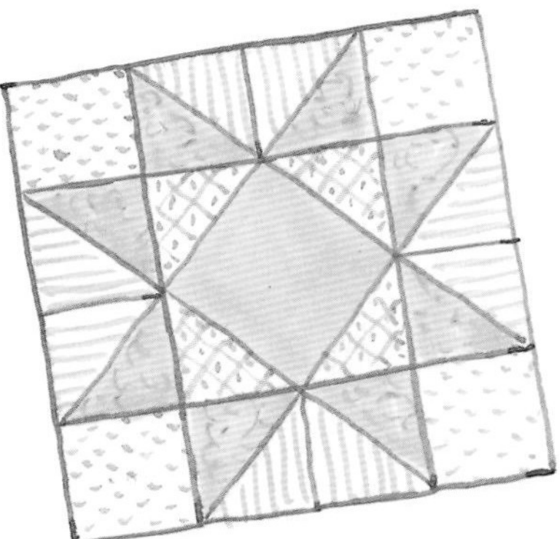

Join the three pieced rows together, matching seams and making sure that the points of the ticking triangles meet the points of the pink square. Repeat the previous steps to make 15 pink-centred stars. Make 10 white-centred stars, following the above procedure but using opposite tones of fabric.

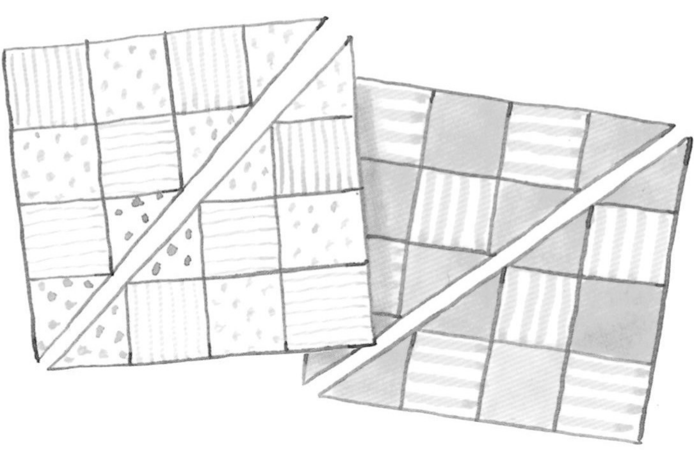

5 Sew eight pink and eight candystripe squares together, alternating fabrics to make a square. Repeat to make 15 squares in all. Cut them in half diagonally, making sure the cut is through the plain pink fabric each time. Repeat step 6 and make 10 squares, this time using the sparsely sprigged fabric and ticking. When you cut the squares diagonally, the cutting line should be through the sprigged fabrics.

6 Stitch a large pieced pink triangle to the left side of a pink-centred star block, then another to the opposite side as illustrated. Repeat until you have stitched triangles on opposite sides of five star blocks.

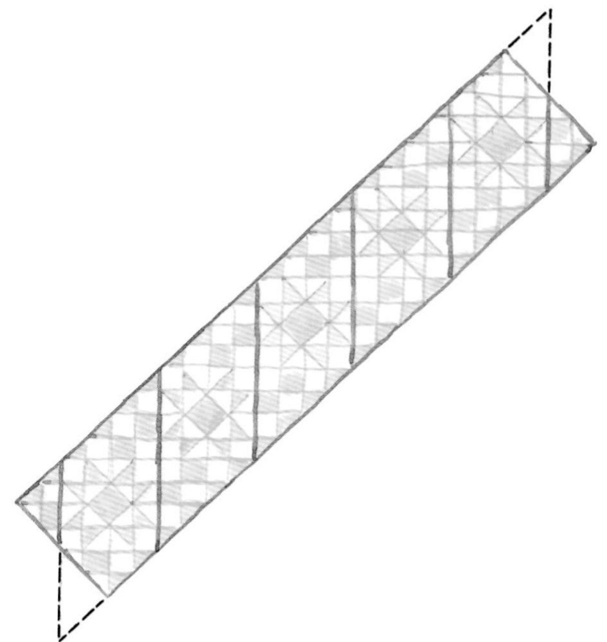

7 Join these sections together, matching seams, to form one row. Cut in half the triangles at the top and the bottom and stitch them to the opposite side of the star block. Repeat steps 6 and 7 to make two further rows of five pink-centred stars.

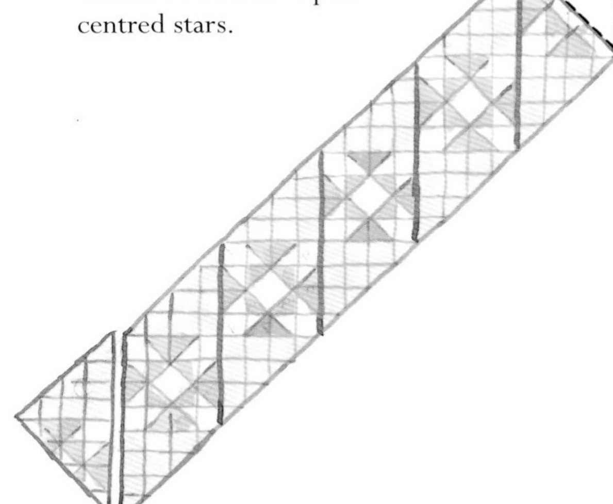

8 Repeat step 6, this time stitching the large pale pieced triangles to the white-centred star blocks. Cut one of the star blocks in half and stitch one half to the top of the row and the other to the bottom. Make one further row of five white-centred stars.

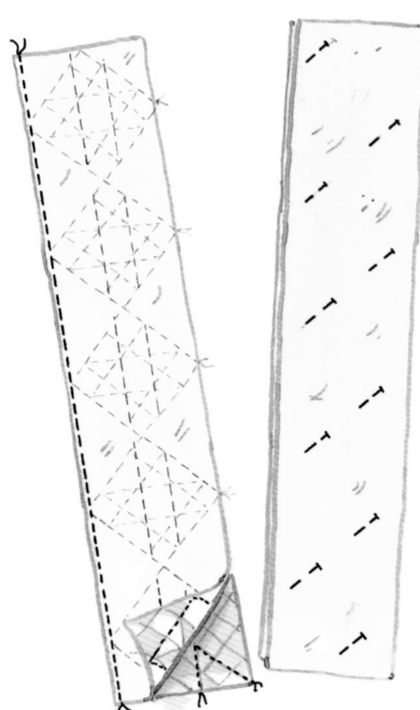

9 Cut five pieces of wadding/batting to the same dimensions as the star rows. Pin and quilt along seam lines. Trim the wadding. Stitch the five rows together. If you want to make the quilt longer, add one border strip of candy-stripe and pink fabric to each end of the quilt.

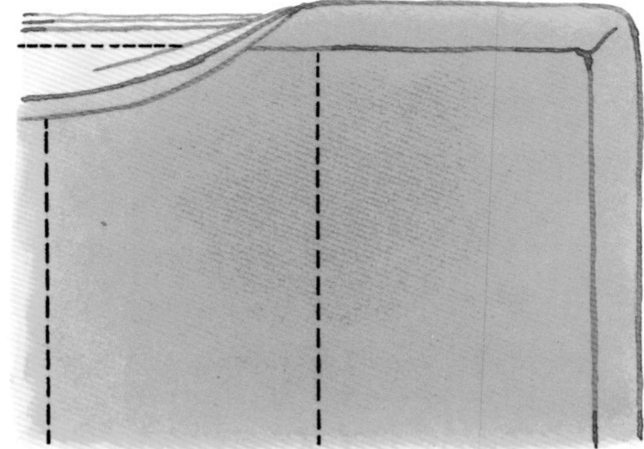

10 Pin the patchwork to the backing fabric and stitch along the four seam lines that join the star rows together. Bind the edges with the pink binding, following the binding strip instructions in the Techniques section.

SQUARE-IN-THE-MIDDLE SINGLE QUILT

This quilt is made up of alternating nine-patch and diamond-in-a-square blocks. To make the quilt into a double-bed size, make it eight blocks wide, rather than seven, giving a total of 64 blocks.

Finished measurements:
2.25 x 2m (89 x 79in)

MATERIALS

- 3 templates, 10cm (4in), 15.5cm (6in) and 21cm (8¼in) square
- 3 striped shirts in medium blues
- 1 striped shirt in pale blue
- 1.25m (1½yd) white cotton sheeting, 2.3m (90in) wide
- 2.5m (3yd) pale blue and white finely striped fabric
- 2.5m (3yd) white cotton sheeting, 2.3m (90in) wide, or white double sheet, for backing
- 5m (5½yd) wadding/batting
- 1 large spool white cotton thread (1000m/1094yd)

PREPARATION

Cut the following pieces:

- **Medium blue shirts**
  28 21cm (8¼in) squares
- **Pale blue shirt**
  28 10cm (4in) squares
- **White cotton**
  56 15.5cm (6in) squares; press each square in half diagonally and cut along fold to give 112 triangles
  112 10cm (4in) squares
- **Blue and white fabric**
  112 10cm (4in) squares
  2 sashes, each 10 x 200cm (4 x 80in)
  2 sashes, each 10 x 225cm (4 x 90in)
  1 strip 4cm x 9m (1½in x 10yd), for binding
- **Wadding/batting**
  cut in half across the width and stitch together along the length

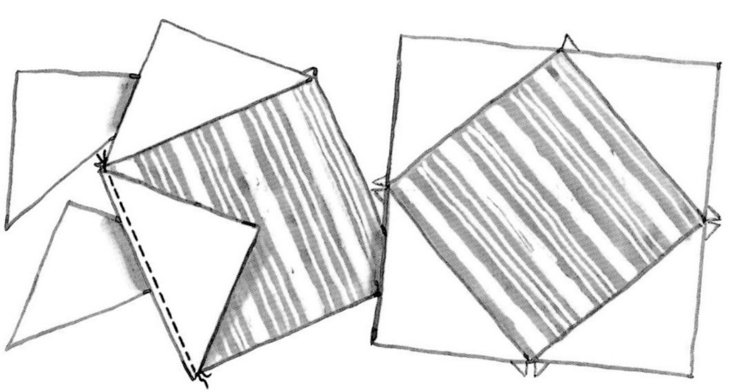

1 To make a diamond block, stitch a triangle to each side of a large square. The points of the triangle will overlap by 6mm (¼in). Remember to press every seam open as you go. Repeat until you have 28 diamond-in-a-square blocks.

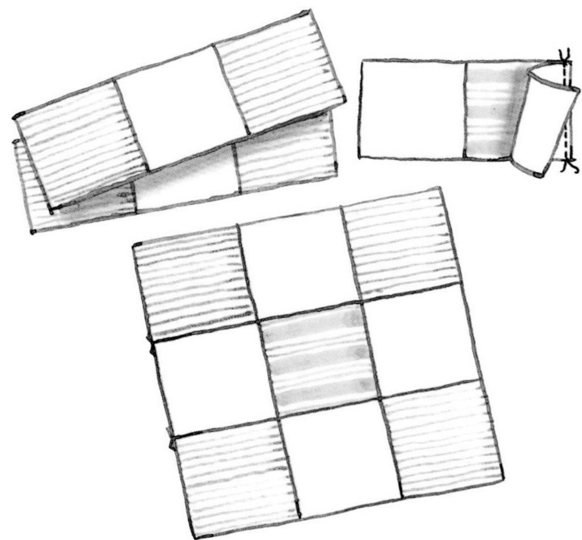

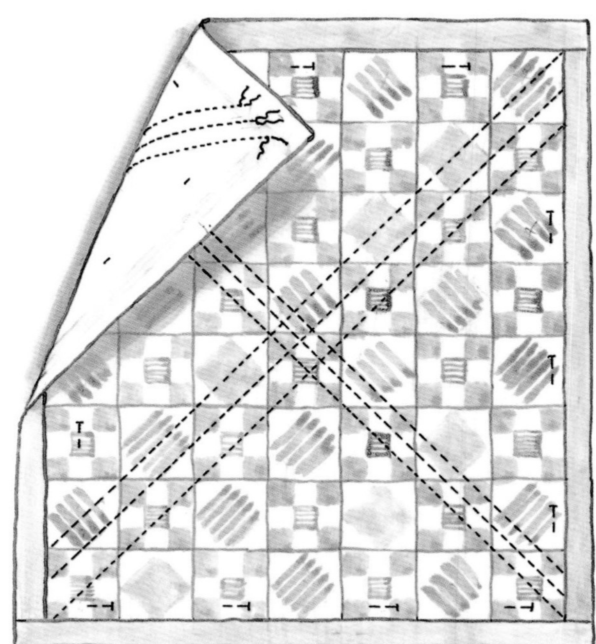

2 To make the nine-patch block, sew a blue and white striped square on each side of a white square. Repeat. Stitch a white square on each side of a pale blue square. Press seams open. With right sides together, pin one of the blue and white striped rows to the pale blue row, matching seams. Stitch. Pin the second blue and white striped row to the pale blue row and stitch. Press.

4 Lay the backing on the floor, wrong side up. Lay wadding/batting on top, then, on top, the patchwork right side up. Pin through all three layers. Quilt diagonally through the squares, starting with the central diagonals and working outwards. If you wish, mark the large squares where quilt lines should go with a water-soluble pen. Trim the wadding/batting and backing.

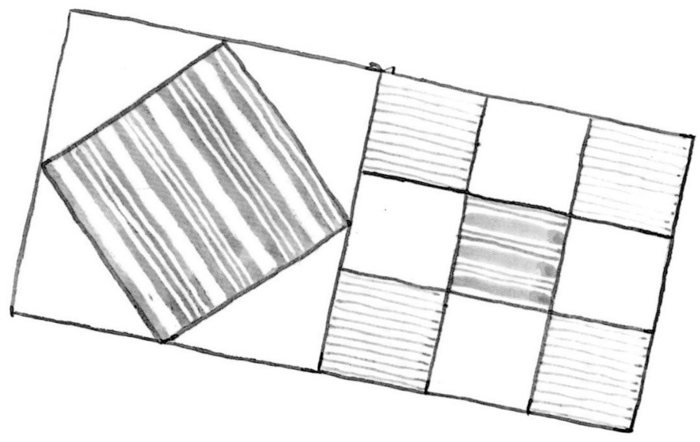

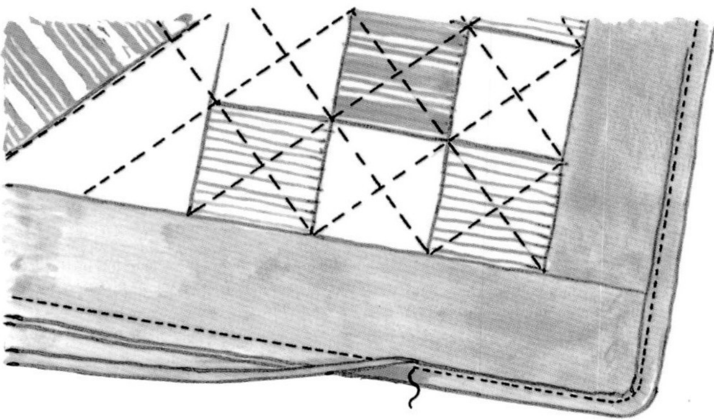

3 Repeat step 2 until you have 28 nine-patch blocks. Make up eight rows of seven blocks, alternating diamond and nine-patch blocks. Stitch together matching seams. Stitch the sashes to the lengths and widths of the quilt.

5 Bind the quilt with the striped strip, following the instructions in the Techniques section for binding with a strip. Make neat pleats at the corners.

DIAMOND-IN-A-SQUARE WALL HANGING

This wall hanging would also make a wonderfully rich bed quilt. Add rows of squares or borders to increase the width or length if required. Old shirts and trousers were cut up and included, but the other fabrics are Liberty country cotton and its famous William Morris lawn print.

The dog-tooth border is optional. For a quicker finish, simply bind the quilt in the usual way, using 5cm (2in) wide strips of one of the left-over fabrics or plain blue fabric.

Finished measurements
(excluding dog-tooth border):
2 x 2.5m (78½ x 98in)

MATERIALS

- 1 template 15cm (6in) square
- 2m (2yd) each of two floral fabrics with a red background (these will also be used as borders)
- 1m (1yd) each of two floral fabrics with a red background
- 1m (1yd) each of five floral fabrics with a blue background
- 2m (2yd) floral fabric with a dark blue background (which will also be used as a border)
- 5.5m (6yd) fabric for backing (either plain or patterned)
- 2.5m (2½yd) plain blue fabric for dog-tooth border (optional)
- 5.5m (6yd) wadding/batting
- red and blue threads

PREPARATION

Cut the following pieces:

- **Floral fabrics**
  187 15cm (6in) squares; place these on the floor to get an idea of how you want to arrange the colours
- **Dark blue floral fabric**
  strips 8cm (3in) wide for borders; you will need 7.5m (8yd) in all, but this can be cut as you sew
- **Red floral fabrics**
  strips 8cm (3in) wide for borders; in all, you will need 11.5m (12yd) of one for the inner borders and 9m (10yd) of the other for the outer border
- **Plain blue fabric**
  (if used)
  strips 20cm (8in) wide for the dog-tooth border; you will need two strips 2.75m (3yd) long and two strips 2.25m (2½yd) long
- **Wadding/batting**
  cut in half across the width and stitch together along the length
- **Backing fabric**
  cut in half across the width and stitch together along the length

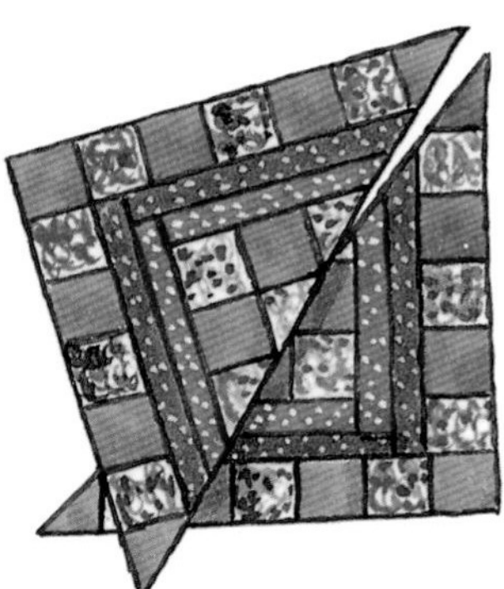

4 Repeat steps 1 to 3 twice more. Now fold these two pieced squares in half diagonally and press. Cut along the fold to make four triangles.

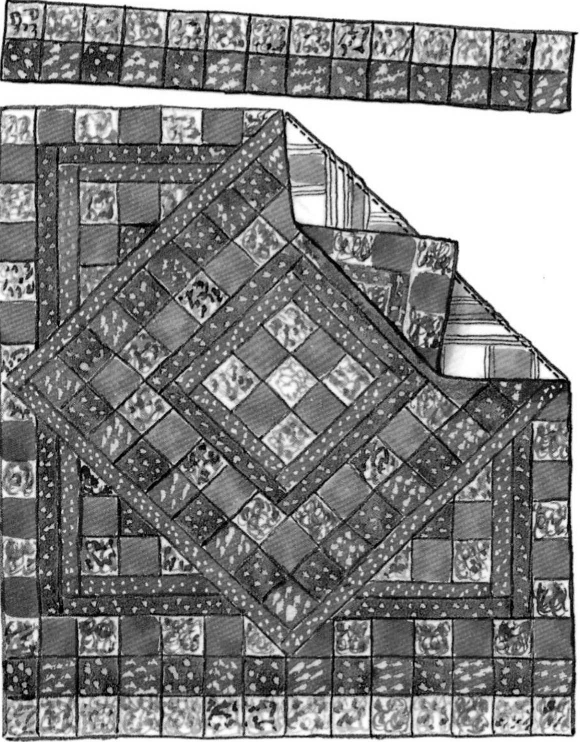

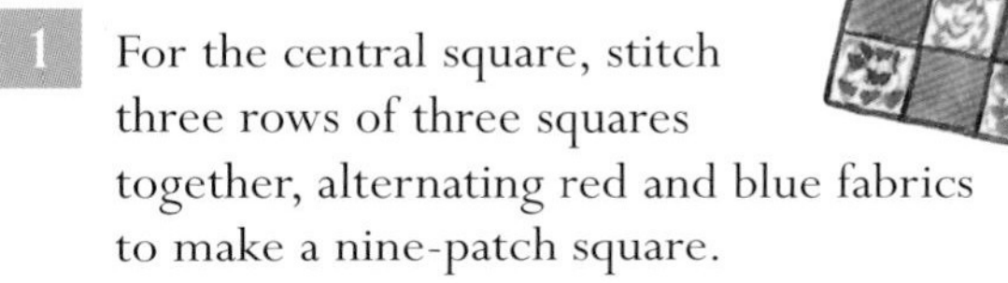

1 For the central square, stitch three rows of three squares together, alternating red and blue fabrics to make a nine-patch square.

2 Stitch a red border strip to the top and bottom of the square and trim. Stitch a red border along both long sides. Repeat with the dark blue border.

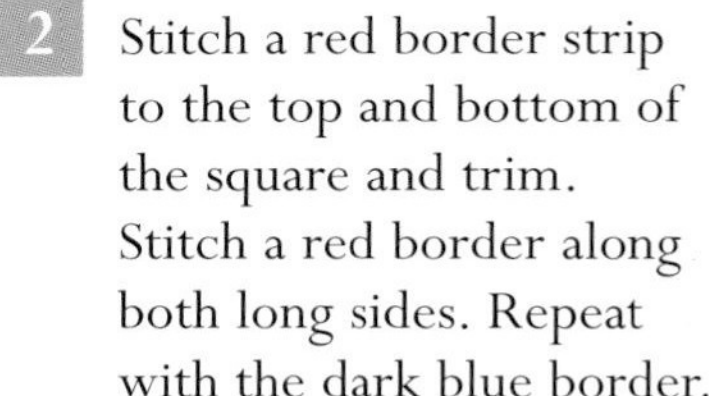

3 Stitch five squares together in a row and attach to one side of the centre pieced square. Stitch another row of five squares to the opposite side. Sew seven squares together and attach to the central square, matching seams where patches meet. Repeat on the other side.

5 Add another row of squares around the central square, using the method outlined in step 3. Surround these with a red border. Attach a triangle, stitching along its base, to each side of the central square. Sew two rows of 14 squares to each end of the quilt, matching all seams. Stitch the red outer border around the patchwork.

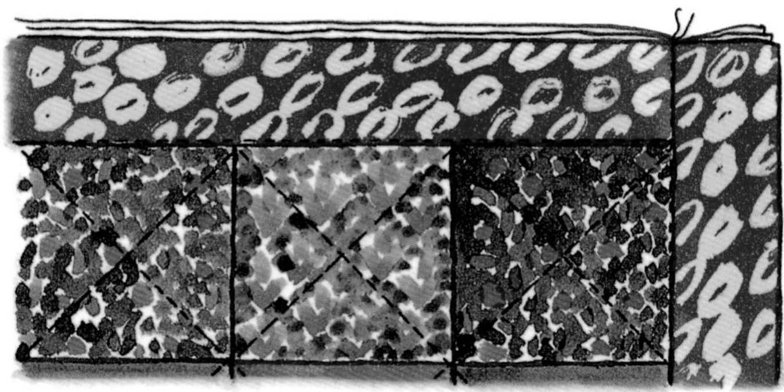

6 Lay the patchwork on top of the wadding/batting and backing. Press, pin then baste into place. Quilt along the seam lines or diagonally through the squares. Trim the edges. Bind in the usual way if you do not want the dog-tooth border.

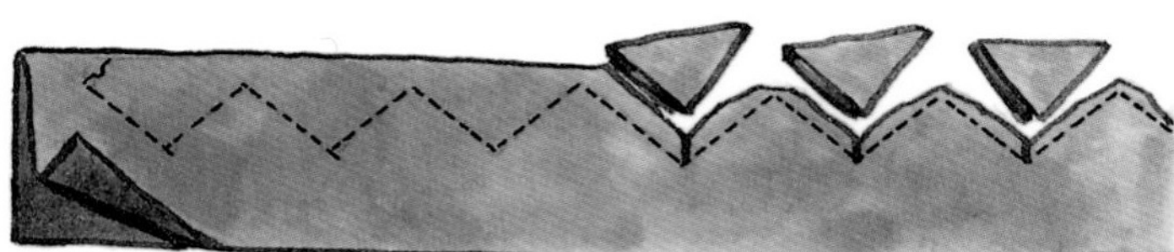

7 To make the dog-tooth border, fold one of the long blue strips in half lengthways, with right sides together. About 6mm (¼in) down from the fold, mark a dot 3cm (1⅛in) from one end and then every 6cm (2¼in) along the length. About 4.5cm (1¾in) down from the fold, mark a dot 6cm (2¼in) from the end of the border, then mark dots every 6cm (2¼in). Sew from dot to dot. Cut triangles out of the folded edge 6mm (¼in) from stitching, clipping at corners. Turn to right side.

8 Stitch the back edge of the dog-tooth border to the wrong side of the quilt, matching raw edges along both lengths. Fold the front of the border to the front of the quilt, fold under the raw edge by 6mm (¼in) and top-stitch just below the previous stitching line. Trim. Repeat steps 7 and 8 with the other long strip, and with the two short strips. Fold the raw edges under at each corner and slip stitch.

TRIP AROUND THE WORLD COT QUILT

This pattern, which comes from Pennsylvania, is also sometimes called Sunshine and Shadow. You will need to follow the diagram closely when you are assembling the quilt. Strips of the fabrics are stitched together into squares, which are then cut into strips. Although the strips sometimes have to be unpicked and reassembled to form the quilt pattern, it is nevertheless not as time consuming as cutting out 289 individual squares and stitching them together.

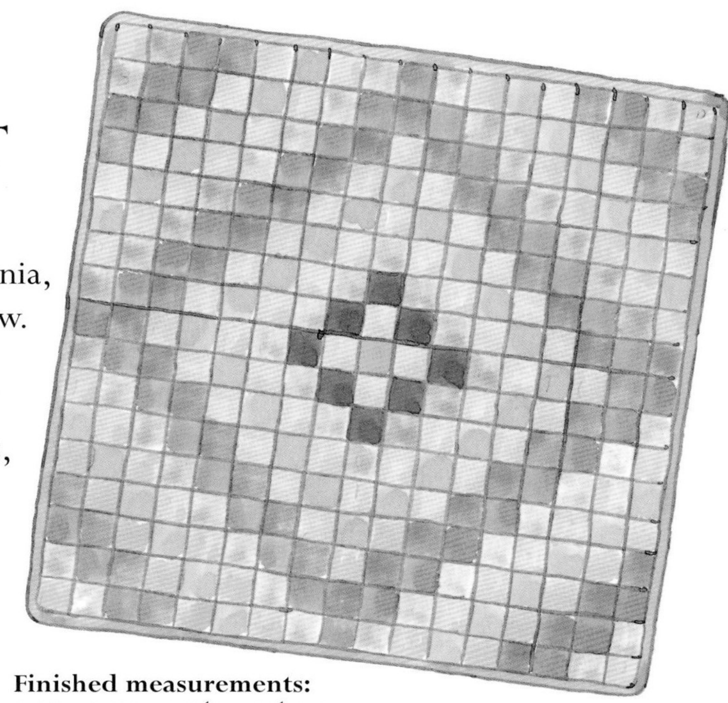

Finished measurements:
1.26 x 1.26m (49½ x 49½in)

MATERIALS

- 1 9cm (3½in) square template
- 50cm (20in) each of six different Liberty Tana lawns, 90cm (36in) wide, three in pinks and oranges and three in blues and lilacs, ranging in density of colour from very pale through to deep pink and blue
- 10cm (4in) dark blue floral lawn
- 30cm (12in) plain mauve lawn
- 2.8m (3yd) plain white fabric
- 2.8m (3yd) wadding/batting
- pale blue thread

PREPARATION

Cut the following pieces:

- **Six floral lawns**
  cut each into 9cm (3½in) wide strips from selvedge to selvedge (you will have five strips in each fabric)
  1 9cm (3½in) square, for the central motif, in the colour of your choice
- **Dark blue floral lawn**
  8 9cm (3½in) squares, for the central motif
- **Orange lawn**
  4 9cm (3½in) squares, for the central motif
- **Mauve lawn**
  cut or tear strips, 4cm (1½in) wide, for the binding
- **White fabric**
  cut in half across the width and stitch together along the length; trim to make a 1.4m (55in) square
- **Wadding/batting**
  cut in half across the width and stitch together along the length; trim to make a 1.4m (55in) square.

Template
enlarge by 200%

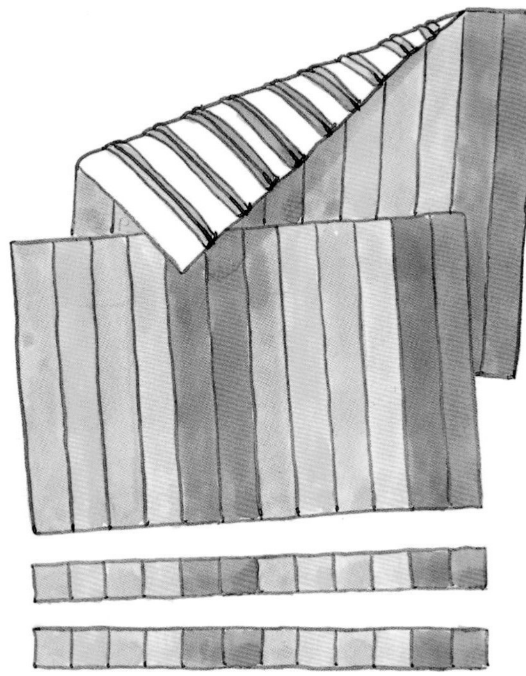

1 Stitch six strips of lawn together, alternating blues and pinks and graduating from pale to darker shades. Add a further six strips in the same order. Repeat with another 12 strips, then stitch the remaining six strips together. Cut across the strips at intervals of 9cm (3½in).

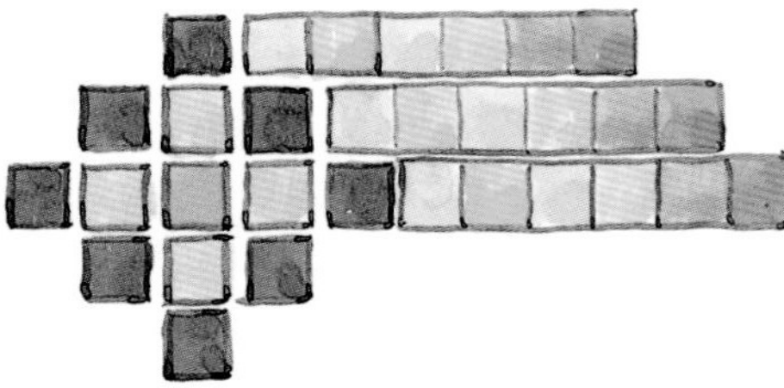

2 Lay out the squares for the central motif on the floor as illustrated. Arrange the rows of squares on the floor around the centre. Follow the diagram and unpick squares where necessary. You will be short of two squares of palest blue squares, so cut the remaining 5cm (2in) strip of that fabric in half across the width and stitch the two halves together along the length. It is now wide enough for your template and the seam will not be visible once the pieces are quilted.

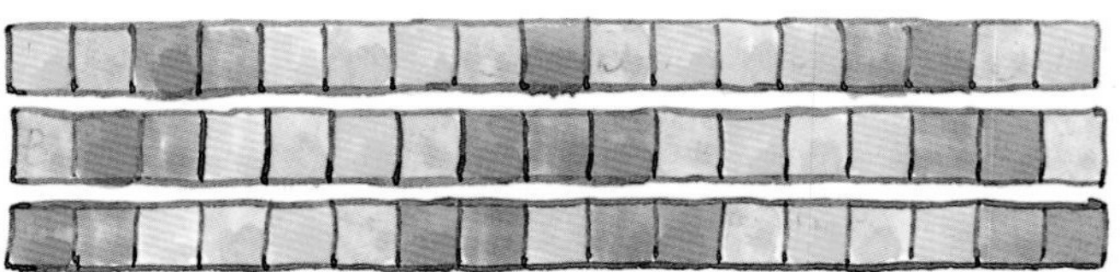

3 Starting at the top of the quilt, join the squares together to make a row. Continue until you have 17 rows of squares, referring to the diagram as you work to make sure that no square is out of place.

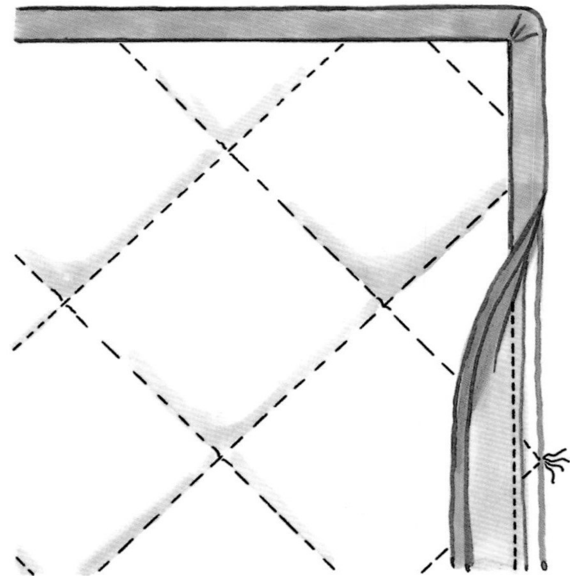

4 Pin the top row to the second row, matching seams, and stitch. Repeat until all the rows have been joined together. Pin the patchwork to the wadding/batting and the backing and quilt with a medium length stitch, working diagonally through the squares. Trim the wadding and backing. Bind the edges with the mauve binding strip, following instructions in the Techniques section.

Amish Wall Hanging

To simplify the making of this wall hanging, you could omit the decorative quilting altogether. Upholstery fabric with a woven-in small motif was used for the hanging shown, and these motifs provided guides for the quilting patterns. When you transfer the star design to the fabric, it is not necessary to trace the whole design; simply mark the inner and outer points of the star and join them up with a light coloured pencil and a ruler, once you have removed the carbon paper.

Finished measurements:
2.22 x 2.22m (86½ x 86½in)

MATERIALS

- large, medium and small star templates; 2 templates, 40cm (15¾in) and 20cm (8in) square
- 2m (2yd) dark red fabric
- 4m (13ft 6in) blue fabric
- 1.25m (50in) green fabric
- 25cm (10in) yellow fabric
- 1 double and 1 single old blanket or 7.5m (24ft 6in) thin wadding/batting
- 7.5m (24ft 6in) black fabric
- dressmaker's carbon paper
- blue, red, green and black threads

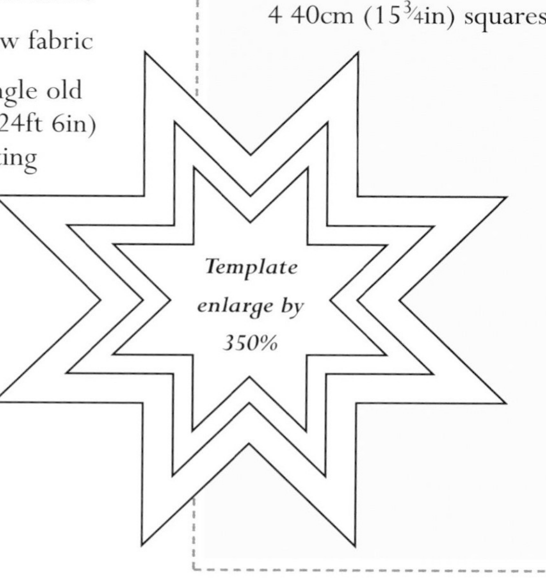

PREPARATION

Cut the following pieces:

- **Red fabric**
  1 82cm (32¼in) square, cut into 4 quarters along the diagonals
  4 40cm (15¾in) squares
- **Blue fabric**
  1 80cm (31½in) square
  4 strips, each 40cm x 1.5m (15¾ x 60in), for borders
- **Green fabrics**
  4 strips, each 20 x 125cm (8 x 49½in)
- **Yellow fabric**
  4 20cm (8in) squares
- **Blanketing or wadding/batting**
  cut out each of the above pieces
- **Black fabric**
  cut 3 2.5m (3yd) lengths and stitch together along the lengths

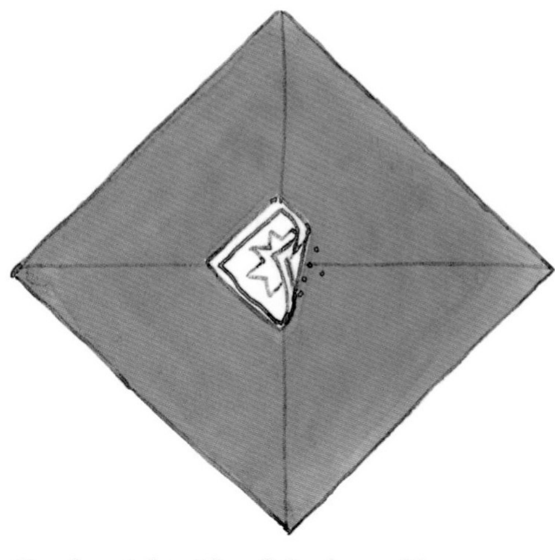

1 On the right side of the large blue square, mark in light pencil the centre lines across the diagonals. Place the star motif in the centre of the square, lining it up with the lines. Slip white dressmaker's carbon paper beneath it and pin. Resting on a hard surface, transfer the outline of the large star to the fabric.

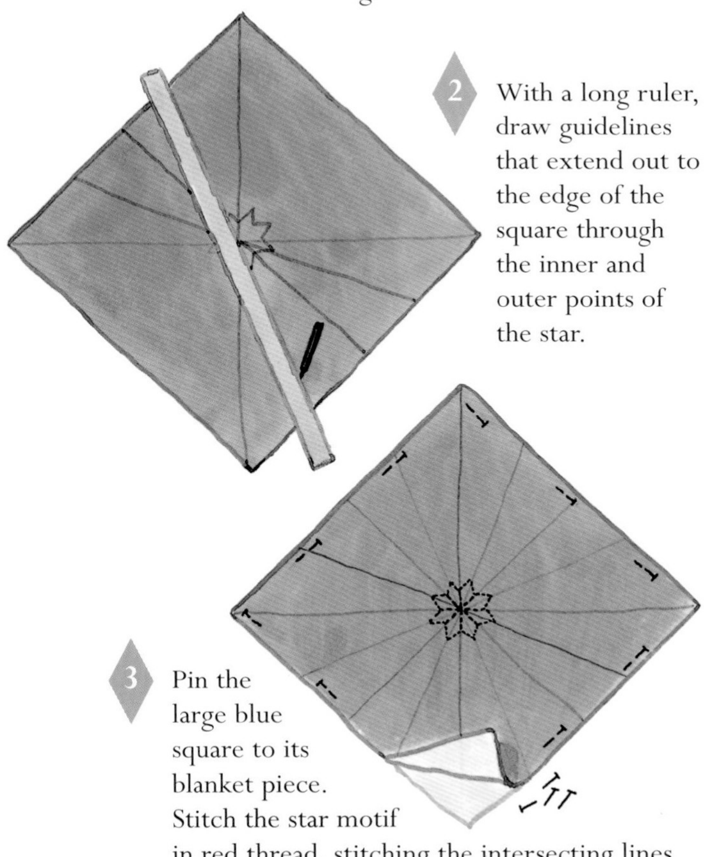

2 With a long ruler, draw guidelines that extend out to the edge of the square through the inner and outer points of the star.

3 Pin the large blue square to its blanket piece. Stitch the star motif in red thread, stitching the intersecting lines first, then the points of the star.

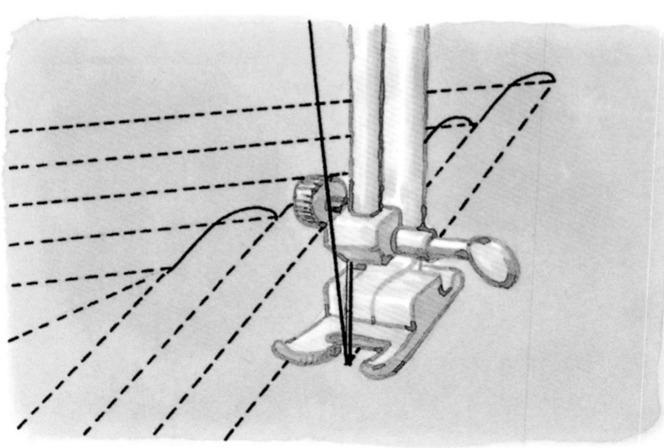

4 With the needle up, raise the presser foot and pull the thread in the machine but do not cut it yet – do that once the entire motif is stitched. Lower the presser foot so that the outside of it is aligned with the first star. Outline quilt around the star, turning corners when the stitching intersects a guideline by raising the presser foot and leaving the needle in the fabric. Continue to stitch around the star 10 more times.

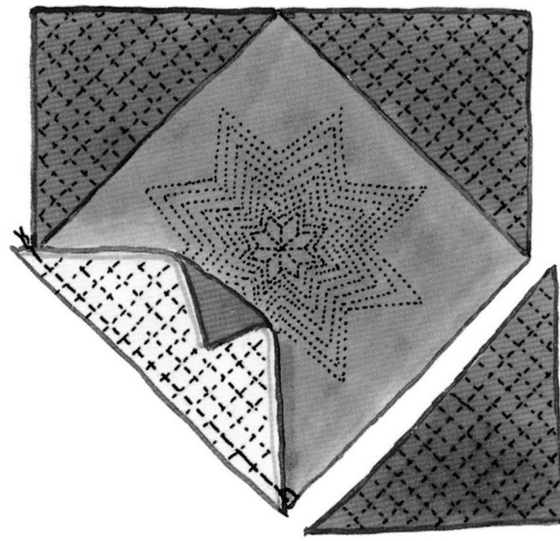

5 Pin the red triangles to their blanket pieces and quilt diagonally, using red thread. The quilting lines should be 2.5–3cm (about 1in) apart. Join the red triangles to the central square.

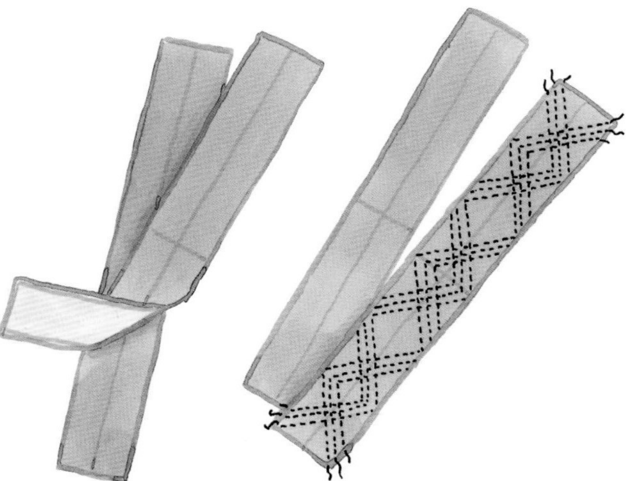

6 Pin the green borders to their blanket pieces. Mark the centre lines across the width and along the length in light pencil. Starting at the mid-point, stitch the pattern as illustrated in green thread, taking care that the triangles intersect along the centre line and keeping the lines parallel and 2.5–3cm (about 1in) apart.

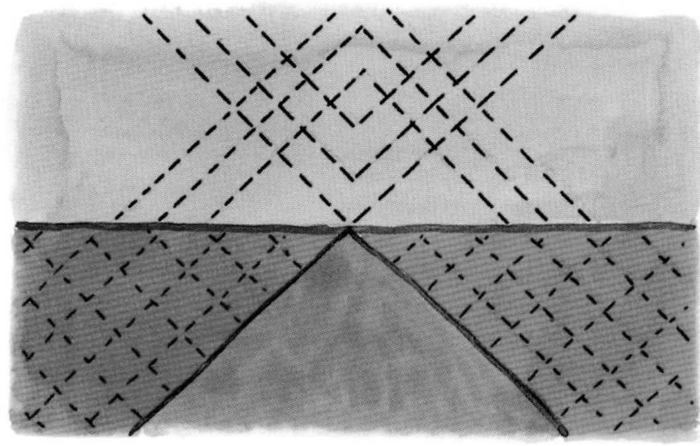

7 Trim the green borders to the same length as the central square, matching the mid-point of the border to the blue diamond point. Pin two green borders to opposite sides of the central square and stitch in position.

8 Mark the medium size star on the centre of the four yellow squares as before, but this time draw the guide lines inside the star. Pin the squares to their blanket pieces and stitch the stars in red thread. Then stitch a line 6mm (¼in) inside the stars.

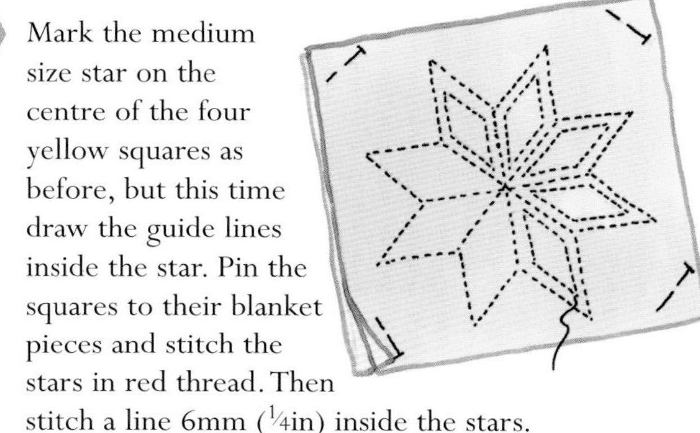

9 Stitch a yellow square at each end of the two remaining green borders. Pin and stitch these to the central square, matching seams and mid-points.

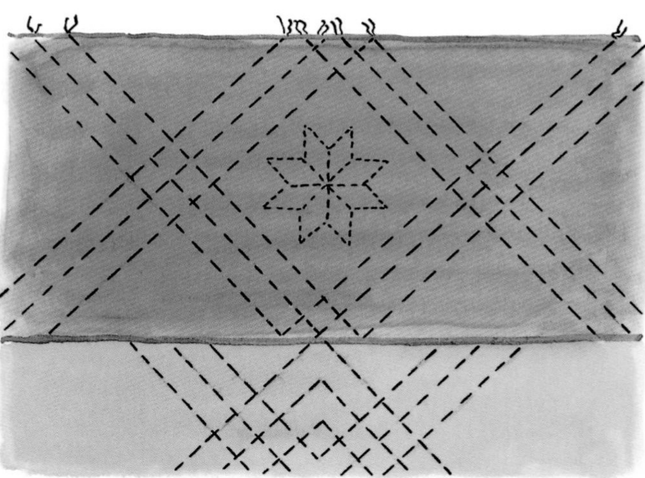

10 Repeat the above procedure with the blue borders and red squares, marking a medium star inside a large star on the squares and a small star at the centre of the blue borders. Follow the pattern as illustrated for the borders.

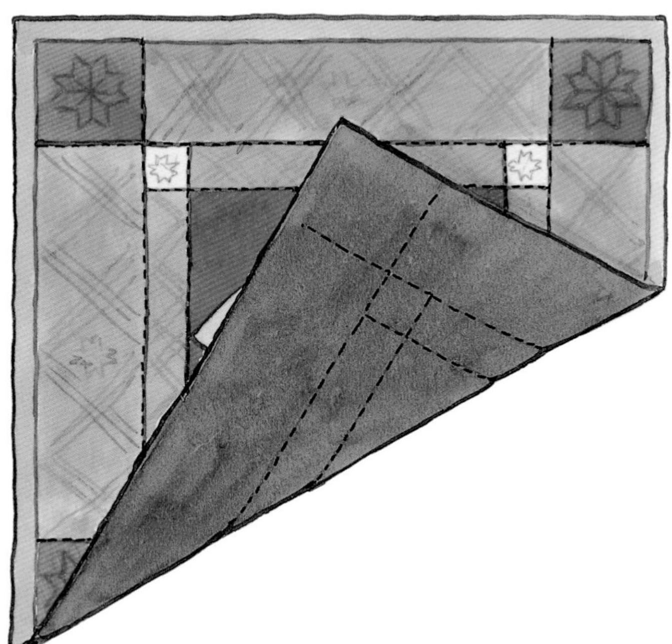

11 With wrong sides together, pin the quilt to the black fabric. Quilt along the seam lines with black thread. Trim the backing to overlap the quilt by 5cm (2in). Follow the self-binding instructions in the Techniques section.

Ocean Waves Double Quilt

When you are making this quilt, it helps if you can visualize exactly how it is built up. It is made up of nine large blocks, which are themselves divided into four smaller blocks, consisting of a lozenge shape of alternating floral and white triangles, with a large white triangle stitched to opposite sides to form a square. Follow the schematic diagram closely as you arrange the different coloured lozenges.

MATERIALS

- 2 templates, 13cm (5in) and 23cm (9in) square
- 1m (1yd) pink floral/abstract fabric
- 1m (1yd) pale blue tiny floral fabric
- 2m (6ft 6in) grey/blue tiny floral fabric
- 5.5m (6yd) plain white fabric
- 8m (8¾yd) plain white fabric, or 2 single sheets, for backing
- 8m (8¾yd) medium weight wadding/batting
- 10m (3yd) pink straight or bias binding, 2.5cm (1in) wide
- 1 large reel white thread
- 1 small reel pink thread to match binding

Finished measurements:
2.58 x 2.58m
(102 x 102in)

PREPARATION

Cut the following pieces:

- **Pink floral fabric**
  48 13cm (5in) squares; press each square in half diagonally and cut along fold to give 96 triangles
- **Blue floral fabric**
  48 13cm (5in) squares; press each square in half diagonally and cut along fold to give 96 triangles
- **Grey/blue fabric**
  120 13cm (5in) squares; press each square in half diagonally and cut along fold to give 240 triangles

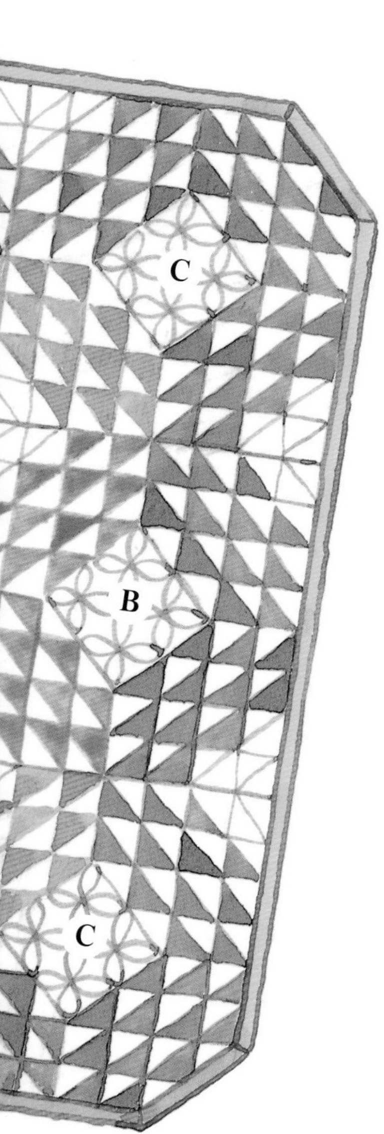

1 To make block A, stitch 10 white triangles to 10 pink triangles along the long diagonal to form 10 squares.

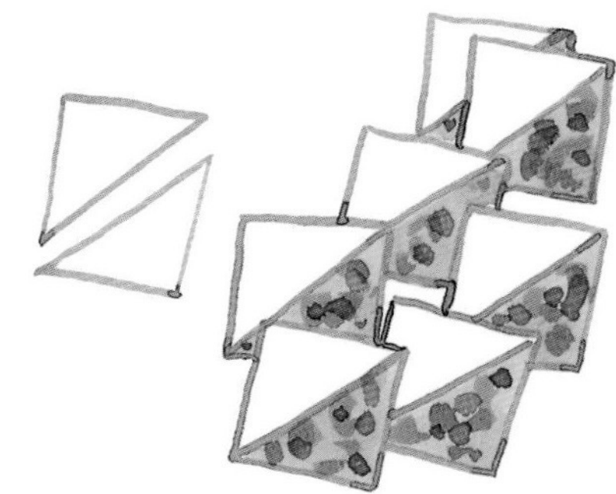

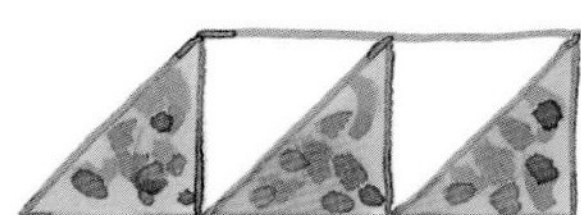

2 To make the first row of the lozenge, stitch two squares together, keeping the white triangles above and to the left of the pink triangles. Attach one pink triangle to the beginning of the row.

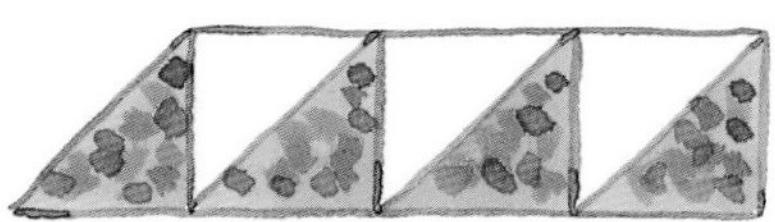

3 To make the second row, stitch three squares together, adding a pink triangle to the beginning of the row as before.

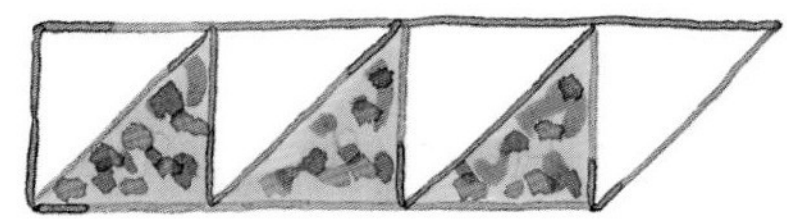

4 To make the third row, stitch three squares together, adding a white triangle to the end of the row.

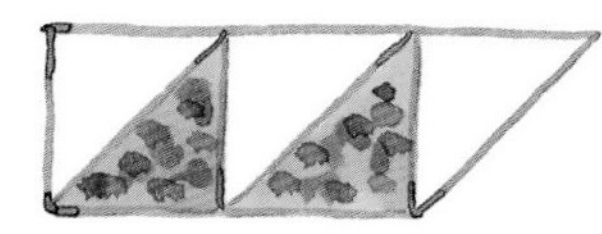

5 To make the fourth row, stitch two squares together, adding a white triangle to the end of the row.

- **White cotton**
  216 13cm (5in) squares; press each square in half diagonally and cut along fold to give 432 triangles
  34 23cm (9in) squares; press each square in half diagonally and cut along fold to give 68 triangles
- **White backing fabric**
  cut into three equal lengths and stitch together; alternatively, stitch the two sheets together
- **Wadding/batting**
  cut into three equal lengths and stitch together

Templates
enlarge by 400%

6 Pin row 1 to row 2, matching seams, and stitch. Repeat with the other rows as illustrated. Stitch two large white triangles to the long edges of the lozenge to form a square.

7 Repeat steps 1 to 6 three more times. Pin two blocks together, matching seams, and stitch. Repeat with the other two blocks taking care that pink and white triangles alternate throughout. Stitch the two rows together so that the large white triangles meet in the centre of block A to form a diamond.

8 To make block B, repeat steps 1 to 7, but this time make two lozenges using the pale blue floral fabric and two lozenges using the grey/blue fabric for each block. Make four blocks in total.

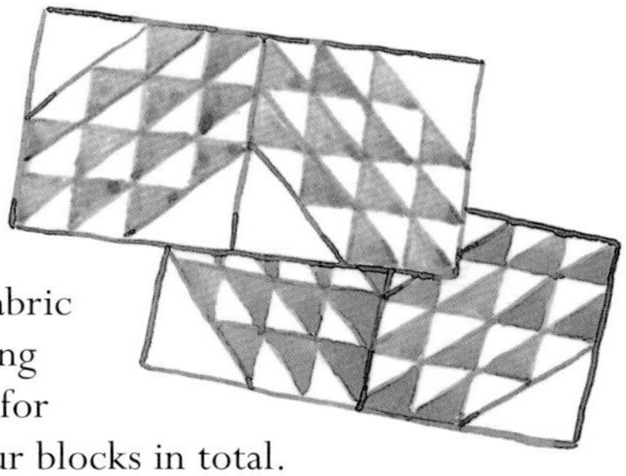

9 To make block C, repeat steps 1 to 7, but this time make three lozenges using the grey/blue fabric and one lozenge using the pink fabric. Omit a large triangle from one of the grey/blue lozenges and position this opposite the pink block when you are piecing the block together. Make four blocks in total.

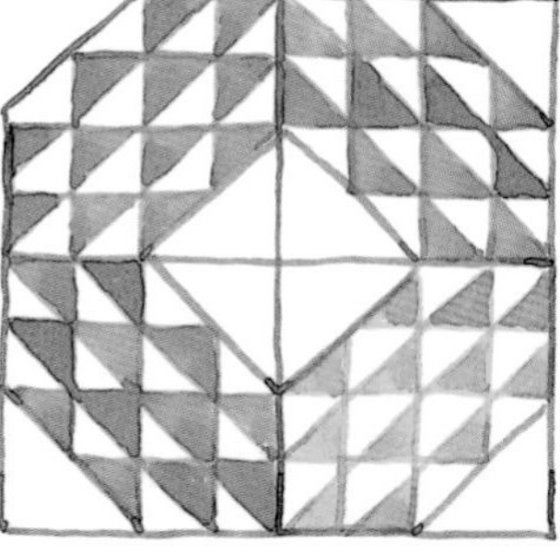

10 Lay block A on the wadding/batting and cut this 1cm (½in) larger than the block all round. Pin or tack the patchwork in place and quilt along the seam lines, beginning with the inner diamond, then quilting all the seams of the pieced block, working from the centre outwards. If wished, continue the quilting lines in to the corner triangles in each direction.

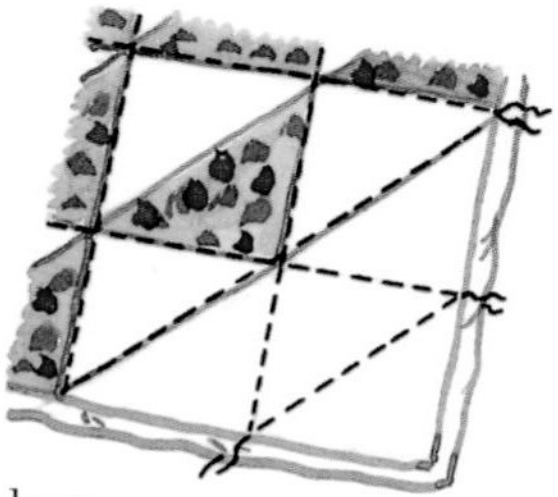

11 Mark dots a quarter of the way along the seam lines of the central diamond to act as guides for the wineglass quilting pattern. Beginning at the centre point, quilt as illustrated, working in one continuous movement. If you are unsure about keeping the pattern even by eye, use a compass and lightly mark the wineglass pattern on the fabric.

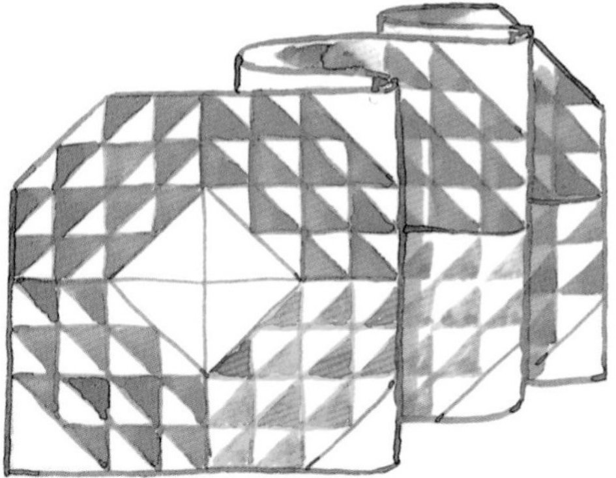

12 Repeat steps 10 and 11 with the eight other blocks. Stitch the blocks together in rows of three, following the quilt layout.

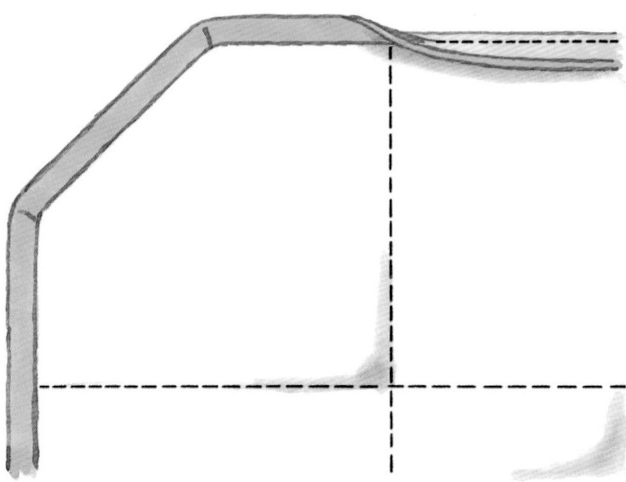

13 With right side up, pin the patchwork to the backing fabric, placing the patchwork so that the backing overlaps slightly all the way round. Stitch together along the seam lines of the large blocks. Trim the quilt. Change the thread in the machine to pink and bind the quilt, following the instructions in the Techniques section for binding with a strip.

English Medallion Quilt

The principle behind this quilt is very simple – plain and pieced borders alternate around an appliquéd central square. The quilt is ideal for commemorating an event such as a wedding, a baby's birth or the centenary of a church – simply alter the appliqué designs to suit the occasion. The fabrics used were mostly discarded clothes, so look out for the next second-hand sale!

Finished measurements:
2.7 x 2.7m (116 x 116in)

MATERIALS

- large and small hearts and petal templates; 3 templates, 15.5cm (6in), 12cm (4¾ in) and 11.5cm (4½in) square; 1 circle template, 1.25cm (½in) radius
- 1m (1yd) green fabric
- 20cm (8in) red tartan
- 30cm (12in) calico
- 2m (2yd) dark blue fabric with flower stripe
- 20cm (8in) red fabric
- 30cm (12in) large red check
- 30cm (12in) red gingham
- 41cm (16in) floral on white fabric
- 70cm (27½in) floral on blue fabric (you could use 2 or 3 different patterns)
- 20cm (8in) blue denim
- 2m (2yd) dark blue with roses (or an old summer dress)
- 2m (2yd) white fabric (an old sheet, preferably with a white on white embroidered design)
- 20cm (8in) green gingham
- 20cm (8in) large dark blue check
- 4 striped shirts in blue, green, beige and red
- 1m (1yd) dark red striped fabric
- 10cm (4in) red fabric with white polka dots
- 11m (12yd) blue and green tartan ribbon, 1cm (½in) wide
- 25m (27½yd) red binding, 2.5cm (1in) wide
- 2 sheets for backing
- 8m (9yd) wadding/batting
- red, blue and white thread

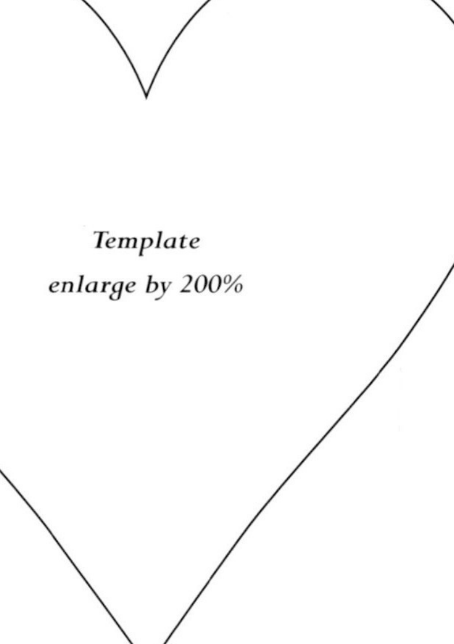

PREPARATION:

Cut the following pieces, cutting or stitching the long strips as you work:

- **Green fabric**
  1 21cm (8¼in) square
  8 11.5cm (4½in) squares
  4 sashes, each 11.5cm x 1m (4½ x 39in)
- **Red tartan**
  4 12cm (4¾in) squares; press each square in half diagonally and cut along the fold to give 8 triangles
  4 11.5cm (4½in) squares
- **Calico**
  4 12cm (4¾in) squares; press each square in half diagonally and cut along the fold to give 8 triangles
  12 11.5cm (4½in) squares
- **Dark blue fabric with flower stripe**
  sashes 15.5cm (6in) wide
- **Red fabric**
  1 large heart, using the template
  4 11.5cm (4½in) squares
  4 15.5cm (6in) squares
- **Large red check**
  12 11.5cm (4½in) squares
- **Red gingham**
  16 11.5cm (4½in) squares
  20 petals
- **Floral on white**
  24 11.5cm (4½in) squares
- **Floral on blue**
  24 11.5cm (4½in) squares
- **Denim**
  4 15.5cm (6in) squares
  4 11.5cm (4½in) squares
- **Dark blue with roses**
  sashes 11.5cm (4½in) wide
- **White embroidered sheet**
  sashes 11.5cm (4½in) wide
- **Green gingham**
  8 11.5cm (4½in) squares
  4 small hearts
- **Large blue check**
  8 11.5cm (4½in) squares
- **Red striped shirt**
  16 11.5cm (4½in) squares
- **Green striped shirt**
  16 11.5cm (4½in) squares
- **Blue striped shirt**
  8 11.5cm (4½in) squares
- **Beige striped shirt**
  12 11.5cm (4½in) squares
- **Dark red striped fabric**
  sashes 11.5cm (4½in) wide
- **Red polka dot**
  60 circles with a 1.25cm (½in) radius from the red polka dot.
- **Wadding/batting**
  cut into three equal lengths and stitch together along the lengths
- **Sheets**
  stitch together for the backing

Templates enlarge by 200%

1 Appliqué the large heart to the centre of the green 21cm (8¼in) square, either with a zigzag stitch or by folding under the raw edges and top-stitching.

2 Stitch eight red tartan triangles to eight calico triangles to form eight pieced squares. Join two pieced squares, with calico triangles together, to form a rectangle with a large calico triangle in the middle. Repeat until you have four rectangles.

3 Sew a green square at each end of two pieced rectangles. Stitch the remaining two rectangles on each side of the central square with the points of the calico triangles pointing inwards. Join the three pieced rows together, matching seams.

4 Cut four dark blue sashes to the same length as the central square. Attach a sash to the top and bottom edges. Stitch a denim square to each end of the two remaining sashes and join to the central square, matching seams.

5 To make the red checked border, stitch seven checked and stripey squares together, alternating patterns as illustrated, and join to the central square.

For the green border, cut four green sashes to the same length as the quilt. Sew two sashes to the top and bottom. Appliqué small green gingham hearts to four calico squares and join one of these to each end of the remaining two green sashes. Stitch these to the quilt.

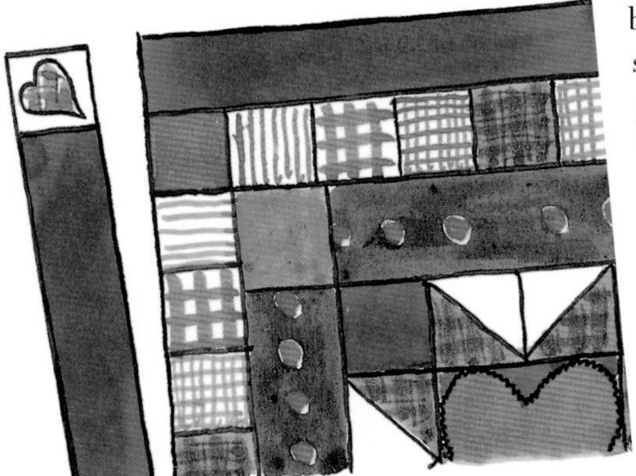

Continue by making a blue floral patched border (top), then a blue rose border with calico corner patches (above), following the layout as illustrated and the method outlined above.

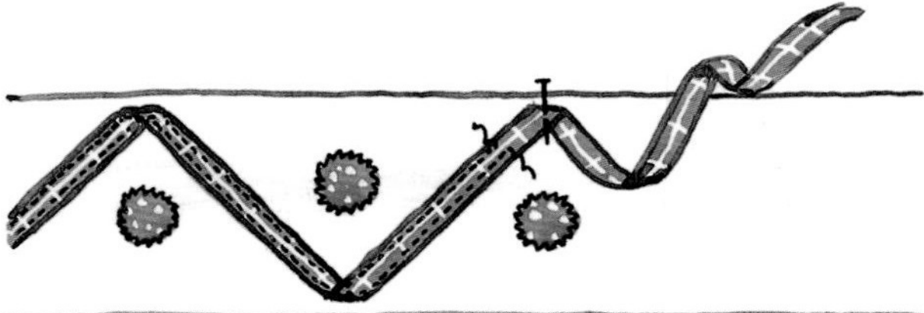

To make the zigzag ribbon border, cut four sheet sashes to the same length as the quilt. On all four sashes mark dots 6mm (¼in) below the top edge at 20cm (8in) intervals, working from left to right. Mark dots 6mm (¼in) from the bottom edge of the sash, 10cm (4in) from the left edge, then at 20cm (8in) intervals. Pin the ribbon to the sash, folding it at the dots. Stitch the ribbon along both edges. Appliqué the red polka dot circles to the white sashes in the centre of the space left by the ribbon.

11 Make a patched border from the shirting, gingham and checked fabrics, alternating the fabrics as illustrated. Join a blue rose border with calico corners to the quilt, then the dark red striped fabric with blue floral corners.

12 Before attaching the white embroidered sheet border to the quilt, make a bow with the remaining ribbon and pin it to the centre of one of the sashes. Fold the ribbon ends to give a streamer effect. Pin in place and top-stitch. Join the sashes to the quilt with or without corner squares.

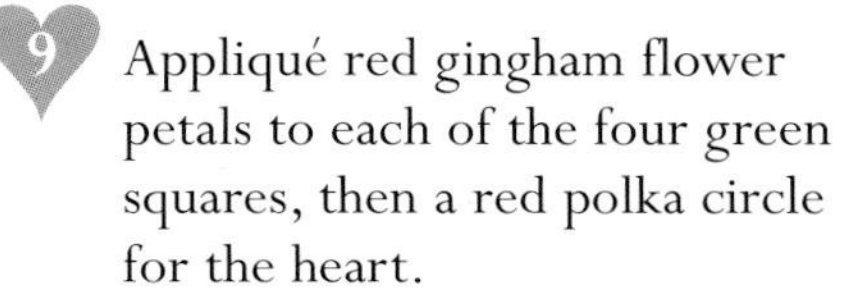

9 Appliqué red gingham flower petals to each of the four green squares, then a red polka circle for the heart.

10 Sew two of the sashes to the top and bottom of the quilt. Stitch the green squares at the ends of the remaining two sashes and join to the quilt sides.

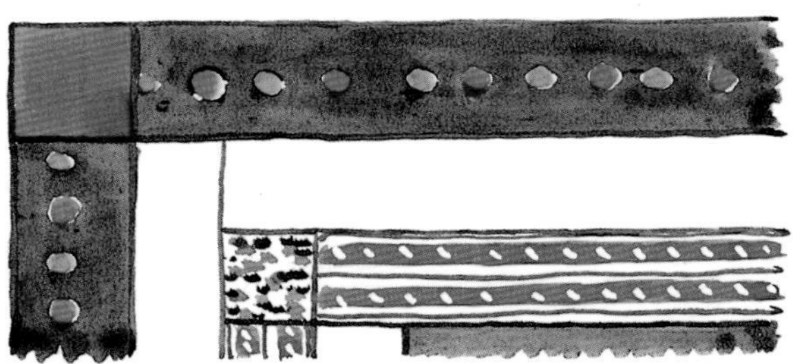

13 Attach the dark blue border to the quilt, and attach red corners. Pin the patchwork to the wadding/batting and backing. Quilt along the seams of each border. Trim the wadding and backing, then bind the quilt with the red binding, following the instructions in the Techniques section.

INDEX

Amish Wall Hanging 111–15

backing 10
bags:
  Beach Bag 25–7
  Evening Bag 22–4
  Little Purse 48–9
  Make-up Bag 32–4
  Overnight Bag 16–21
  Rucksack 28–31
batting 10
Beach Bag 25–7
binding 12
  binding with a strip 13
  decorative binding 13

Child's Skirt 44–7
corners 14
cosies:
  Egg Cosy 58–9
  Tea Cosy 56–7
Cot Quilt, Trip Around the World 108–10
Crazy Patchwork Cushion 70–71
cushions:
  Crazy Patchwork Cushion 70–71
  Log Cabin Cushion 67–9
cutting 9

decorative binding 13
Diamond-in-a-square Wall Hanging 104–7
Doll's Shoofly Quilt 72–5
Drawing Room Throw 79–81

Egg Cosy 58–9
English Medallion Quilt 122–7
equipment 8
estimating fabric lengths 7
Evening Bag 22–4
Evening Star Double Quilt 96–100

fabrics:
  choice of 7, 10
  cutting 9
  estimating lengths 7

Hairband 51–2
hanging quilts 14
hangings, wall:
  Amish Wall Hanging 111–15
  Diamond-in-a-square Wall Hanging 104–7
  Kilim Wall Hanging 92–5

Jacket, Sleeveless 38–43

Kilim Wall Hanging 92–5

Little House Picture 53–5
Little Purse 48–9
Log Cabin Cushion 67–9
Log Cabin Throw 85–8

Make-up Bag 32–4
Mat, Place 60–61
materials 7–8
Medallion Quilt, English 122–7

Nine-patch Single Quilt 89–91

Ocean Waves Double Quilt 116–21
Ohio Star Single Quilt 82–4
Overnight Bag 16–21

patches, piecing 9
Picnic Rug 76–8
Picture, Little House 53–5
piecing 9
Place Mat 60–61
Provençal Tablecloth 62–6
Purse, Little 48–9

quilts:
  Doll's Shoofly Quilt 72–5
  English Medallion Quilt 122–7
  Evening Star Double Quilt 96–100
  Nine-patch Single Quilt 89–91
  Ocean Waves Double Quilt 116–21
  Ohio Star Single Quilt 82–4
  Square-in-the-middle Single Quilt 101–3
  Trip Around the World Cot Quilt 108–10
quilting 11

Rucksack 28–31
Rug, Picnic 76–8

Scrunchy 50
self-binding 12
Shoofly Quilt, Doll's 72–5
signing quilts 14
Skirt, Child's 44–7
Sleeveless Jacket 38–43
Square-in-the-middle Single Quilt 101–3

Tablecloth, Provençal 62–6
Tea Cosy 56–7
techniques 9–14
templates, making 8
threads 8
throws:
  Drawing Room Throw 79–81
  Log Cabin Throw 85–8
Trip Around the World Cot Quilt 108–10

wadding/batting 10
Waistcoat 35–7
wall hangings:
  Amish Wall Hanging 111–15
  Diamond-in-a-square Wall Hanging 104–7
  Kilim Wall Hanging 92–5